CHURCH AND RACE IN SOUTH AFRICA

CHURCH AND RACE
IN SOUTH AFRICA:

*Papers from South Africa, 1952-57,
illustrating the churches' search for
the will of God*

EDITED BY

DAVID M. PATON

SCM PRESS LTD

56 BLOOMSBURY STREET LONDON

1958

First published July 1958

Printed in Great Britain by
Northumberland Press Limited
Gateshead on Tyne

CONTENTS

CONTENTS

PREFACE

PEOPLE outside South Africa get South Africa and South Africa's tragic troubles thrown at them from time to time in the headlines; but it is often difficult for us to see how the situation to which the headline draws our attention arose, or to imagine how our fellow-Christians in Africa are seeking to come to terms with it.

The documents that follow, selected from a far greater number, are presented as an attempt to help people outside South Africa to gain a greater and more compassionate understanding of the struggle of the Church with the Race problem in South Africa. They are presented with only such editorial comment (printed in italics) as I have judged necessary to make the contexts clear. Dates are given and, where only a part of a document is included, this is noted. The selections from the Charges of the Bishop of Johannesburg to his Diocesan Synod for the years 1952 to 1957, review the principal events; Mr. Grant's account of the fortunes of Adams College is in narrative form : the two together may assist the reader who is hard put to it to place in their correct sequence the various successive measures of the Nationalist Government of the Union of South Africa, to understand something of the background of the shorter statements towards the end of the book.

I am extremely grateful for the permissions, readily given, to reprint these various papers; and for help and advice in preparing the book, so generously given by people who really do know something about South Africa.

We who are not South Africans are inclined to see in South Africa only the Race Problem; and perhaps also to judge the Church in South Africa solely by what we take to be its faithfulness or otherwise in seeking for and doing the will of God in respect of this particular problem—a problem so much more taxing than any that most of us have had to encounter. But it may be doubted whether it looks like that to South Africans—or to God.

7

Partly because they offer me a chance to express my gratitude for his *Cry, the Beloved Country*, and partly because they may remind us of common weaknesses and recall us to common loyalties, I should like to quote some words of Dr. Alan Paton at the All-Africa Christian Conference in Nigeria, in January, 1958:

'A Christian may be conservative or reformist, and still be a Christian. But he stands unequivocally for the supra-temporal goods which the temporal order must cherish. Furthermore, he is aware of sin, both in himself and in others; he sees his opponents as men and women who, like himself, are creatures of God, and what is more, are dear in his sight, and therefore not fit subjects for tyranny. I do not believe that Christians always know what is best to do, and I certainly do not believe that they will agree with one another. But on one thing, and the most important thing, they should be agreed, namely the nature of the foundation on which the good society should be built.

That is our task, to witness to these things, humbly because we are sinners, confidently because we are citizens of that continuing city of which our Lord is the Master and the King.'

Easter Week, 1958.   DAVID M. PATON

SELECTIONS FROM THE
CHARGES TO HIS DIOCESAN SYNOD
OF THE
RIGHT REVEREND
RICHARD AMBROSE REEVES
BISHOP OF JOHANNESBURG

Ambrose Reeves has been a secretary both of the Student Christian Movement and of the World's Student Christian Federation and later Rector of Liverpool. He has been Bishop of Johannesburg since 1949.

1952

As we gather year by year in Diocesan Synod, much of our time of necessity is occupied with the domestic affairs of the Church in this diocese. Yet, important as it is for us to take counsel on those matters which concern the maintenance of the work of the Church, none of us can escape the fact that we are meeting at a time when the skies of our national life are darkened by the clouds of uncertainty, bitterness and fear. As representatives of a great body of churchpeople through-out the Southern Transvaal, we are bound to take cognisance of the setting within which the Church has to live and do its work. This we must do, neither because we have any desire to obtrude ourselves into spheres which properly belong to the State, nor because we have a ready-made solution for any of the many problems confronting South Africa, but because so much that is now happening in our land is grievously afflicting so many of the people committed to our care. Just because we believe the Church exists in this world to be the agent of God's

A*

purpose, we cannot accept the suggestion that any human interest or activity ought to lie outside our concern.

SUPPRESSION OF COMMUNISM ACT

In June, 1950, I expressed my disquiet at the measure then before Parliament for the suppression of Communism. Since then, this measure has become law, and to-day it is far easier than it was then to see how it is going to work in practice. Little that has happened in these last months has brought any reassurance. The grave dangers that would result from taking the punishment of Communists outside the normal processes of law if those who are accused of being Communists are to be denied recourse to the normal courts of the land are far more apparent than they were two years ago. For centuries now it has been demonstrated that the only guarantee of freedom for the individual is the rule of law. Once the free access of all citizens, whatever their offence may be, to the courts of the land is denied, then human freedom is placed in jeopardy. For those who are accused of being Communists to be deprived of their livelihood and restricted in their movements at the dictate of the Minister responsible would, if such a thing comes to pass, be a situation which ought to alarm all who care for freedom. Not that we underestimate the seriousness of the challenge of Communism. It is probably the most formidable competitor for the allegiance of man that the Church has ever had to face in its long history. But our point is that the type of legislation which has been passed in our country to deal with this menace is such that it can only succeed in driving Communism underground, and in the process is denying to those accused of being Communists that justice which all citizens have the right to expect. On a short-term view, this Act may ostensibly accomplish that which it was designed to do, but in the long run it will have other and very different results from those which its authors intended. Surely all the time and energy which is now being used to implement this Act could be much better employed in promoting justice in the complex multi-racial society in which we live, and in attempting to change the many social conditions in South Africa which are providing just that breeding-ground for Communism in which the Marxists delight. This latter task is one which ought to concern us all, for in some degree we are all responsible for the fact that there are so many defects, mischiefs and abuses in contemporary society. While on the one hand it is our Christian duty to create good citizenship and loyalty to lawful authority, on the other hand we must criticize and challenge tyranny and injustice wherever we meet it. We ought to be deeply ashamed if we acquiesce dumbly in things as they are.

EUROPEAN HOUSING

This I believe is especially the case if we consider the cruelty that is being inflicted on masses of people by lack of housing, by overcrowding, and by the slum conditions in which they have to live. Here is a matter on which the consciences of all the faithful need to be quickened, for the state of affairs is so shocking that it calls for immediate and bold action. It is almost unbelievable that in a city such as this in which there is such wealth, European families can be found who are condemned to live in garages. But such is the case, for there is an acute housing shortage. We are told that at the present time there are at least 3,000 European families in urgent need of accommodation. Such shortage is leading in some cases to the break-up of families, children having to live apart from their parents with 'in-laws', child separated from child, with the consequent deterioration in the morale of the family which we should expect. In some cases women who see their families compelled to live in hovels in which there is no privacy are taking to drink to try and forget their troubles. Bad housing and overcrowding are damaging to health of body, and sometimes to health of mind and soul. Surely it is time that as Christians we addressed ourselves seriously to attempt to remove this scandal from our social life.

AFRICAN HOUSING

When one turns to the question of African housing, or rather the lack of it, the situation can only be described as appalling. It is estimated that in Johannesburg alone 50,000 houses are required to meet the present shortage of houses for non-Europeans and that a further 29,800 houses will be required in the next ten years. These figures take no account of the shortage of 21,700 houses in the Reef towns and the estimated need for an additional 20,000 houses there during the next ten years. Within the area of this city and the Reef there is a present shortage of 71,700 houses, and an estimated future need for 49,800 houses, making a grand total of 121,500 houses. Yet statistics by themselves may do little more than impress upon us the immensity of this problem. We must bring our imagination to bear on this vast issue, so that we see it not merely in terms of houses, but in terms of the human suffering that is being caused this and every day to thousands upon thousands of human beings in our midst by the lack of adequate housing. Surely it is time that this matter was taken completely out of the realm of party politics and considered on its merits, quite apart from any theoretical and academic consideration of race and colour.

That the Dutch Reformed Churches suggest trying to do this very thing by calling a conference of representatives of all the churches in South Africa to discuss this and similar questions, is a matter of great encouragement to all those who are troubled in conscience about these things. Here is a human problem of the first magnitude crying out for a solution. For such a solution to be found we are convinced that the first requirement is that all Europeans should face the fact that the urban native is here to stay. It is to deny the realities of our situation to pretend that he is in transit from kraal to kraal. He is an integral part of our urban society; an essential and valuable part of the labour force without which no industrial community in South Africa could persist. As such he deserves decent housing, adequate transport to and from work, and wages which will enable him to keep himself and his family in a reasonable fashion. As far as the city of Johannesburg is concerned, it is difficult to avoid the conclusion that, apart from all the financial and technical problems involved in tackling such a vast problem, there is a strange lack of will on the part of those in authority to get to grips effectively with this crying need when one learns that in 1951, 83 houses were built in this city for Africans as against 1,763 houses built in the Reef towns during the same period.

But here again it is all too easy for us to blame others for such an unsatisfactory state of affairs. After all, those in authority represent the European citizens, and it is difficult to believe that they would persist in their present irresolution in the face of a problem of such magnitude, unless they were confident that the Europeans in this city are generally content to leave things as they are. It is difficult to speak for others, but I am persuaded that if churchpeople, even though they are a minority in the population, were brought to realize the tragic effects upon human life of the present vacillation and indecision, something would be done and done speedily. In the face of this situation, I would urge all parochial councils and the organizations in every parish to study carefully the facts of the situation in their own city or town, and, after educating themselves, to make whatever representations they conclude are necessary to the municipal, provincial and national authorities and to persevere in their efforts, refusing to be silenced.

COLOURED PEOPLE'S HOUSING

Compared with the Africans and Europeans, our Coloured people are a relatively small community. But their position is just as serious. In one Coloured township alone, there are a thousand families waiting for houses. In regard to the Coloured people, side by side with the problem of the shortage of housing, is the fact that to-day there is considerable unemployment. I learn that there are 1,400 men and women registered as unemployed, but the probability is that unemployment is more widespread in the Coloured community than these figures suggest. Certainly we must not overlook the problem and needs of our Coloured people, as we think of the distressing conditions in which so many have to live in urban society.

The Bishop also spoke of political tensions and the Christian; of the building of new churches; and of the Diocesan Mission.

1953

The Bishop began by speaking of the Diocesan Mission, and then continued:

TRADE UNIONS

CERTAINLY it ought not to be difficult for us to realize that God has set us to live in evil times, for there is so much happening around us in the world that must cause Christian people to be disquieted. And what is true of the world in general, is true of South Africa in particular. There are three matters which are causing concern to many thoughtful people to which I would direct your attention. The first is the present uncertain position of many of the Trade Unions in South Africa. It is now many years since Pius XI asserted in a famous Encyclical ' Not only is man free to institute these unions . . . but he has the further right to adopt such rules and regulations as may best conduce to the attainment of the end in view.' And in our own communion, as long ago as 1919, the Archbishops' Committee on Christianity and Industrial Problems declared in its report—' Experience suggests that unrestricted competition among workers and among employers tends to result in social degradation, and that trade associations, including all workers, both men and women, in each industry, and similar associations, including all employers, are the best foundation of mutual understanding, industrial peace, and social progress.' To-day the effectiveness of trade union organization is being threatened from two directions. In the first place, some of the European unions are being deprived of effective leadership by the naming of a number of their leading officials under the Suppression of Communism Act. It is hard to believe that all of these men and women, many of whom have held positions for years of great responsibility in their unions, are adherents of the Communist party. Possibly, some of them flirted with Communism at some stage in their career, but even if they did, the very fact that no indication is given of the evidence against them, and that a growing number of trade union leaders have been summarily deprived of their livelihood on the order of a Cabinet Minister is gravely unjust. Nobody is more anxious than I am that the errors of Marxism should be combatted, but the use that is now being made of the Suppression of Communism Act gives the impression that those in authority are attempting to paralyse the legitimate activities of certain sections of organized labour. The fact that those who are removed from their positions in the Trade Unions have no right of appeal to the courts of the land only adds to the misgivings many have over the application of the legislation. Nobody would question that the Minister is doing anything other than administering the law, but the fact is that this legislation is thoroughly bad, for it places more power in the hands of the Minister than any human being ought to have over his fellows. Here is a law which goes far to abrogate the rule of law in certain circumstances and for particular individuals, and as such deserves the strongest condemnation from any who care for the maintenance of justice in man's dealing with man.

The effectiveness of trade union organization is also being threatened in the second place by the determination of those in authority to ignore African trade unions. No doubt such unions are at present few and relatively weak, but that is understandable, for the movement of Africans into industry is comparatively recent. Further, it is true that so far they have not been prohibited. But the fact that those in authority are circumventing such unions by setting up legal machinery for dealing with just those matters for which trade unions exist instead of encouraging the growth of strong trade unions among African workers is bound to reduce the existing unions to impotence, and make it impossible for African workers to organize themselves as they ought to have every right to do. I am afraid that many people consider that this is no concern of theirs because those affected belong to another racial group. So easily are racial matters allowed to cloud and obscure an issue which properly belongs to the ordering of the organization of workers in the industrial field.

The Bishop then spoke of the Bantu Education Bill which had recently been passed by Parliament, and of its effects on Mission Schools (this is also the subject of The Liquidation of Adams College) *and then of the Western Areas Removal Scheme and its implications for African property rights (issues which have been memorably treated in Fr. Trevor Huddleston's* Naught for Your Comfort). *He concluded . . .*

THE VOCATION OF THE CHURCH

The difficulties at present confronting the trade unions in this country, the problems that are raised for the Church by the proposed changes in African education, and the future of the Western Areas are all matters with which we, in common with all who care for the welfare of all peoples in South Africa, are bound to concern ourselves. But even as we make our comments on these or any other proposals which affect our common life, we do well to remember that we are called to redeem the time. Though the times in which God has set us are such that we may easily be borne along on the general tide, it is possible for us to ransom this present time from loss or misuse, releasing it from bondage to evil, and claiming it for the highest good. As St Paul reminds us, in the same passage to which I referred earlier : there is a Divine purpose making for good in the midst of evil : a purpose which we can perceive and follow. That purpose is made known to us in Holy Scripture. In the Old Testament we learn that the purpose of God is selective, calling, choosing and sending a people to be the instrument of His purpose. And the New Testament shows us that our Lord Jesus Christ, having recreated the people of God by His own person and His own perfect obedience, having also chosen the twelve, sent and sends the Church to embody and continue His mission. Into that Church we have all been incorporated. Now it is our duty and our privilege to allow the Holy Spirit so to work in us that we may be fashioned into the Body of Christ and filled with power. Here is the way in which we must redeem the time : by becoming the Church : by being in fact the mystery of the gospel that we proclaim.

PRACTICAL CONSIDERATIONS

All of us, no doubt, are aware that of late the Church of the Province has been severely criticized by some of our friends overseas for failing to make a sufficiently bold stand against injustice and oppression in South Africa. It would be very easy for us to dismiss many of their criticisms as being ill-informed and to pay little or no attention to most of them. But it might be better if we asked ourselves how far we are redeeming the time in the life of the Church here in South Africa, and particularly in the kind of situation of which we have just been thinking together. Certainly we do have occasions, such as at Synod, when on a diocesan level members of our Church express their unity in Christ, whatever may be the particular racial group to which they may happen to belong. Again, we recognize that for geographical, linguistic and other reasons it is most suitable that normally members of the Church should worship in their own racial groups. But we need to be most vigilant lest what is agreed upon as a matter of convenience becomes elevated into a principle under the pressure of certain views which are now so powerful in our country. Further, the very difficulty of the times in which we are living suggests to me that we ought to be doing much more than we are on a parochial level to help the ordinary members of our congregations to realize their unity in Christ. Not that I am urging that we should try in some artificial way to bring this about. But let us not forget that in the Church, and here I am only speaking of our life in Christ in His Church, we are either growing together or we are drifting further apart from one another. I am convinced that if only we were more sensitive than we sometimes are of the need that there is for members of different racial groups to grow together in the Church, we should find that occasions would arise quite naturally from time to time when members of a parish and a mission ought to meet together. For example, there might well be some matter upon which a parochial and adjacent mission council ought to consult one another; some special celebration when the priest from a parish or mission district should be invited to the other's church; some piece of work that might profitably be undertaken together by a mission and neighbouring parish; some festive occasion when members of both congregations might worship together. I realize that occasionally there is such contact as that which I have indicated, and I know that people cannot be forced to worship, work and take counsel together. But my point is that as occasion makes it possible, we ought quite naturally to take every opportunity God gives us for our African, Coloured, and European Christians to grow together in the Body of Christ. Here in South Africa we have striven for over one hundred years to draw men and women of diverse races into one Church, giving to all a share in the government and administration of that Church. As I look back over the history of the Church of the Province I can find no justification for allowing the spirit of racial sectarianism to creep into the life of the Church.

1954

The Bishop began by surveying the triumphs and difficulties of the Church in the Diocese, and went on to speak of the Anglican Congress at Minneapolis and the Second Assembly of the World Council of Churches at Evanston, both of which he had attended.

BANTU EDUCATION ACT

REFERENCE to this report leads me to comment on certain aspects of our present situation which arise out of those racial prejudices and fears which impair so many of our relationships with one another, and which are now in process of being entrenched in the laws of the land. In particular I would speak of two matters, both of which affect most directly those of our churchpeople who are of African race. But I make no apology for speaking to all churchpeople on these questions, for those of us who do not belong to this particular racial group would make a fatal mistake if we concluded that they do not concern us. It may well be that if we acquiesce passively in what is now taking place, we shall in effect be conniving in the undermining of those values of civilization that we cherish, and by our silence be encouraging policies which in the long run may easily affect us more adversely than our African brethren. Indeed we must expect that to happen, for any policies that assume that civilization can only be preserved by regimentation and restriction are bound sooner or later to sap the courage and vitality of those who have to implement such policies.

For this reason I would direct your attention to ' The Bantu Education Act'. All of us realize by now that under this Act we are bound to lose practically all our schools. Let us say quite frankly that when we examine the educational views of those responsible for this piece of legislation, we have no desire in these circumstances to retain our schools. We have no wish to have any part or lot in a system of education, the main purposes of which were expressed when the Bill was introduced in such words as these: 'Education must train and teach people in accordance with their opportunities in life according to the sphere in which they live. Good racial relations cannot exist when education is given under the control of people who create wrong expectations on the part of the Native himself.' It was then declared that 'Native education should be controlled in such a way that it should be in accord with the policy of the State.' Moreover, we are bound to pray and work for the repeal of this Act, because it is a very clear example of the type of legislation which leads to despotism, conferring as it does almost unlimited powers on the Minister of Native Affairs. This is resulting in the Bantu Education Act being administered through a succession of circulars over which Parliament has no control. But the loss of these schools places a heavy responsibility upon the Church. Now we must intensify the religious education of African Anglican children within the Church. This may be a blessing in disguise, for in recent years we have been inclined to rely too much upon the schools to carry out this important piece of work. Now we have no option in the matter, for we are now compelled as a Church to make far more adequate provision than we have hitherto done for the religious training of the coming generation of churchpeople. This is a tremendous task which will tax our resources greatly, for we have both to secure an adequate supply of African men and women who are willing to make the sacrifice necessary to teach children in Sunday School, and who are ready to give the time that is needed if they are to be properly trained for this important work. Yet I cannot conceive of any more worthwhile task for any to undertake who care for the Church, and who long for those who come after them to be built up into the great Anglican heritage that is ours. So I would appeal to those who are disturbed by what is now happening in the field of African education, and who have the ability to help, not to sit down in despair. Still less ought they to waste their time and energy in fruitless criticism of the secular authorities. Let them offer themselves to their parish priest and get on with the job. If they do this, then what seems now to be a grievous loss, may well be a great gain. Whether this be so or not, at least we shall have the satisfaction of knowing that in our day and generation we did all that we could to secure that the children God has entrusted to His Church were not forsaken by us in their hour of need.

MISSION CHURCH LEASES

Secondly, I would ask you to consider the instructions that have been issued to local authorities informing them of the conditions which must be inserted in all leases offered in the future to churches desiring to erect buildings in locations. While there is a certain ambiguity in the language used, it seems clear that the Minister of Native Affairs reserves to himself the right to deprive any church of the opportunity of working among the African people if he considers that the occupier or his representative engages in activities which the Minister regards as outside the normal scope of church work, is guilty of any words or actions which lead to a deterioration in the relationship between the government and the African people, or engages in any subversive activities. There is no need for me to dwell on the significance of such terms, for they must be apparent to us all, even if we do not realize the gravity of the issues now raised for the Church. It would, of course, be possible for the Church to refuse to accept such grievous conditions, but the consequence would be that we should be prohibited from erecting new churches in urban areas at the very time when there is an urgent need for us to expand our work in such areas. Further, if the Church decided to do this, it would mean that as existing leases of churches fall in, we should be compelled to close the churches concerned. To adopt such a course would be to act irresponsibly towards our people. All that we can do is to accept the conditions now suggested, recognizing that, while none of us would wittingly engage in subversive activities, we must continue to declare the truth as God has given us to see the truth. That we must continue to do, whatever may be the consequences. As I see it, we have no alternative as ministers of the gospel, even though I am aware of the grave responsibility of so deciding. A decision which is all the more grave because I realize that it may mean that churches will be closed by the authorities in the State, and for a time, at any rate, devout members of the Church will be deprived of the ministry of the Word and Sacraments. But, unless we are prepared to stifle our consciences, and remain silent in the face of injustice and wrong, there is nothing else that we can do. It is tragic to contemplate, but I cannot believe that those who would suffer most if they were deprived of buildings in which to worship would wish us to remain silent. What is equally serious is that by remaining silent, we should be failing to exercise the duty that the Church has in every age of examining the plans and policies of men in the light of Christian principles and of pointing out when such plans and policies are in conflict with those principles. Of this we may be assured: The Church will be the stronger for our action. As T. S. Eliot has said, the Church is 'triumphant in adversity. It is fortified by persecution: supreme, so long as men will die for it.' At the same time, I would plead with all whom God has called to leadership in this diocese to speak and act at all times responsibly, with a full sense of the consequences of their words and actions to others as well as to themselves. Provided that is done, we can leave the issue in God's hands, confident that He is able to care for His own. Because this is our faith, we shall not keep silent in the face of the grave injustices and wrongs of the present, unless or until we are silenced.

WESTERN AREAS

But, important as these particular matters are to all church-people, because of their far-reaching implications for the life of the Church, we must not overlook the fact that there are a number of other issues which, at the present time are causing particular concern to many African churchmen. For example, there is the question of the threatened mass removal of the inhabitants of the Western Areas. The fact that we have discussed it on various occasions in the past is no reason why we should fail to bear it in mind in the present. Few people would question the advisability of removing families who are living in overcrowded and insanitary conditions, and either demolishing or putting in order slum properties. Indeed, we have long urged that this should happen, not only in the Western Areas, but also in Shanty-town in Moroka, and in the Orlando shelters, where such steps are long overdue. To allow such terrible conditions to continue as those obtaining at present in the Orlando shelters is a crime against humanity. Yet, while we deplore the existence of such conditions, we have opposed and shall continue to oppose in every legitimate way the uprooting of the whole population in the Western Areas, together with the deprivation of the freehold rights which some there have enjoyed for many years, all of which is undertaken merely to implement a particular racialist ideology.

The Bishop's final passages concerned Segregation in the Universities; and the task before the Church in South Africa.

1955

IN my travels during the last two years both in the United States and Great Britain it has been apparent that many people are oppressed by danger of war. Large numbers of people are aware that the bomb that was dropped on Hiroshima on the Feast of the Transfiguration, 1945, taken in conjunction with the strides made since then in nuclear research, mean that mankind has moved into an era in which perils hitherto undreamed of now threaten the human race. For example, it has been calculated that the atomic weapon exploded at Bikini last year had six hundred times the destructive power of the bomb that was dropped on Hiroshima. This gives us some idea of the ghastly dangers now confronting all nations, for nuclear weapons have an unprecedented power of destruction. The position is made much more dangerous by the fact that so far all attempts to forbid or control the use of such weapons have failed. Faced with such possibilities of destruction on a vast scale it is imperative that Christians everywhere should persevere in their prayers for peace, and both work zealously for the removal of the deep-seated legacies of envy, fear and hatred left by past wars, and do all that they can to counter the mischievous propaganda which stirs up so much ill-feeling between the nations. In addition we have a clear duty at all times to recall men everywhere to the law and judgment of God, so that they may come again to recognize that all human authority rests upon and is limited by that body of commandments which express the will of God with regard to human conduct and which have either been implanted by nature in the human mind, or are capable of being demonstrated by reason. Once this law of nature is ignored, men believe that their own power is absolute, and that the only function of the laws promulgated by earthly rulers is to express the will of those who are in power. Then justice begins to decay, and in the end disaster is bound to overtake the life of a nation.

OBEDIENCE OR DISASTER

Christians to-day have to make up their minds as to whether, under any circumstances, it is ever justifiable to use these nuclear weapons of destruction. This is one of the most difficult questions that confronts us in this generation. For my part I find it difficult to visualize any circumstances in which a nation would be morally justified in unleashing such terror upon its enemies, even by retaliation. While it is true that historically the church has always regarded injustice as a greater evil than war, it is questionable if this agelong attitude can be maintained in a nuclear era. Realizing the unprecedented dangers which now threaten the peace of the world, surely we ought to be ready to unite with Christians everywhere in calling for an international agreement banning weapons which, if they are used, might easily destroy civilization, reduce the treasures of the past to dust, and cause human suffering on a scale that is beyond our power of imagination.

THE CHALLENGE OF COLOUR

It is understandable that many people in all parts of the world are preoccupied with the perils of nuclear warfare. But there is a danger that such a preoccupation with the possibility of war may blind them to, and distract us from, the serious issues raised for this generation by the ever-increasing demands of one thousand, seven hundred million coloured peoples in the world upon the seven hundred million economically dominant white people. It may well be that the peace of the world depends as much upon the answers that are given to the questions raised by this issue, as it does on discovering how Communist and non-Communist may co-exist on the same planet. Indeed a bold policy for feeding the starving millions of Asia and the undernourished millions of Africa in present circumstances, might well be a better insurance against war, than by continually piling up greater and greater stocks of atomic weapons. At any rate, as far as Africa is concerned, and in particular South Africa, much that is now happening is fertilizing the soil of African life in such a way that it will be all too easy for the seeds of conflict to grow and flourish in the coming days. Not that the question of race relations is confined to the continent of Africa. At a time when the coloured people of the world outnumber the white people by almost three to one, and in which the members of the different racial and cultural groups are being brought into ever closer contact and communication with one another, racial issues are becoming almost a universal problem. Such a situation makes it inevitable that the white and coloured people of the world will have to make radical readjustments in their attitudes to one another if they are ever to learn to live together in peace. It is the difficulties that arise in trying to do this very thing which gives rise to the so-called 'colour problem', and which result in differences of material welfare, culture, and economic development between the members of various racial groups becoming hopelessly confused with racial differences. This confusion in turn gives rise to manifestations of colour prejudice, racial discrimination, and social separation. By such means many people in many parts of the world seek to resolve their own conflicts and to deal with their own anxieties. In fact, a great deal of racial tension is the result of a deep sense of insecurity and the fear of losing a particular social status in society.

THE CHALLENGE FOR SOUTH AFRICA

At the same time, the fact that this is one of the most stubborn problems facing the whole world at this time, does not excuse any of us from directing our attention to this issue. On the contrary, the fact that those at present in authority in South Africa claim that they have a plan which will deal satisfactorily with these questions makes it specially incumbent upon Christians in the Union to scrutinize their proposals with great care. On the occasion of previous Diocesan Synods we have dealt at some length with various attempts by the authorities in South Africa to express their racial theories in legislation. We have seen more than once in these last few years that however sincerely the authors of such legislation may have desired to do nothing more than differentiate between those of various racial groups, the effect in practice, has been to discriminate against the non-European. Time will show, I believe, that this is also true both of the Bantu Education Act and the Senate Act.

CHURCH FAMILY CENTRES

Let us look at the Bantu Education Act for a moment. For a proper understanding of this piece of legislation it must be taken in conjunction with the report of the Native Education Commission appointed in 1949, and the speeches made by those responsible for framing this Act. It was the effect of all these taken together which led the Bishops of the Church of the Province last year to condemn the Bantu Education Act in no uncertain terms. Convinced that the intention of this legislation was to provide a form of training which would fit those who received it to take their place in an uncivilized tribal community life, I decided in November of last year that we could in no way, however remote or indirect, assist the authorities in carrying out such a policy. Since our schools closed in March last, we have opened Church Family Centres in ten mission districts in which we have twenty full-time paid African workers. This project has been entirely financed by money specially given for this purpose by the Society for the Propagation of the Gospel, the Africa Bureau, private subscribers, and most recently by a gift of £2,000 from an overseas trust. Although the Church Family Centres have only been in existence for a few months, valuable service is being rendered to some fifteen hundred Anglican children, as well as many young people and adults in those districts. Here good is certainly coming out of evil, for although we are prohibited from giving formal education in these centres it is clear that in them we have an instrument which can be used for building up our African churchpeople into the Church and of rendering increasing service to them in the coming days. We are admittedly still in the experimental stage, but I would commend this venture to the continued and earnest prayers of all churchpeople throughout the diocese.

LEVY FOR BANTU EDUCATION

Before leaving the Bantu Education Act we are compelled to draw attention to the two shillings a month which is being added to the rent of Africans dwelling in new urban townships in order that schools may be provided in these areas. It is extraordinary that the imposition of a discriminatory tax of this nature has passed almost unnoticed. To the average white person such a sum no doubt seems trifling, but for many Africans it is far from being a negligible amount. It is of course the natural consequence of having pegged the amount from general revenue available for African education, but this does not make it any more morally defensible. On the contrary, the principle of a special levy upon the poorest section of the population to provide for their educational needs calls for the strongest possible condemnation.

THE SENATE ACT

In some respects the Senate Act is the most grievous thing that has yet happened in the sphere of legislation, not so much because it deprives large numbers of European voters of representation in the Senate, though that in itself is alarming enough. The serious thing is the action proposed to remove the Coloured people from the common roll. In a sense this is a measure of greater racial intolerance than anything that has been done to the African, for it is an action against a group of people who would not exist if it had not been for the presence of White people in South Africa. They are a people whose interests have traditionally been bound up with those of the White racial group, and this forcible separation of them is bound to increase bitterness in the Union and to cause further international questionings.

APARTHEID POLICY?

Yet all this legislation can only be understood in its proper context if, as I said earlier, we direct our attention seriously to the policy of compulsory segregation which is being so assiduously followed in South Africa at the present time. We cannot escape noticing that this is happening at the very time when determined efforts are being made in many parts of the world to remove the political, economic and social disabilities from which the Coloured people have suffered so long. Equally determined attempts are being made here to segregate those in the various racial groups from one another in order to perpetuate the continued domination of the White minority in South Africa. Without question the exponents of this policy sincerely desire also to contribute to the welfare of racial groups other than the White one, but we must not be under any illusion that their main purpose is the preservation, at all cost, of White domination. For this reason we ought to examine calmly and seriously this basic concept of *apartheid* which lies behind all the present policies in South Africa. Yet we at once are confronted with the difficulty which is caused by the varying connotations that are given to this word by different people. In its idealized form of total separation, the policy of *apartheid* looks forward to the time when there will be completely self-sufficient African communities in South Africa. Most people recognize that such a separation involving giving up all Black labour with the tremendous economic consequences that would result from taking that step, make such a proposal quite impracticable. White and Black are too clearly bound up together in our economy for such a course to be possible. The very fact that there is a growing labour shortage is in itself a sufficient deterrent for such a proposal. If the economy of South Africa is to go on expanding we shall have to learn that the proper alternative to cheap, insufficient, unreliable African labour is not to do without it, but to see that it becomes efficient, willing and dependable, with a far higher standard of living than obtains at present.

TERRITORIAL *APARTHEID* IMPOSSIBLE

The same is true of geographical segregation. It is quite impracticable to return most Africans to the reserves for these areas cannot maintain the population at present living in them. This is one of the notorious facts which is so often overlooked. Further, one of the major misconceptions propagated by the exponents of geographical segregation is that there are irreconcilable differences between the culture of the African and the European. None would deny that, at present, there are deep cultural differences between them. At the same time, it is sheer nonsense to pretend that all Africans are irrevocably divided from Europeans by their tribal affiliations, language and social habits. On the contrary, increasing numbers of them are becoming inextricably interwoven into the life of the white community. We need to recognize that total segregation and geographical separation are both completely impossible in South Africa.

The fact is that the only form of separation and segregation which can be applied in South Africa is the form which we are experiencing at the present time; a form of racial sectarianism which is leading slowly but surely to a rising tide of anger against the white man, and which is making co-operation among the different racial groups increasingly difficult.

RACE RELATIONS ARE HUMAN RELATIONS

Behind present policies there lies the assumption that 'racial tensions are brought about when members of different races live in juxtaposition and that it is in the interests of racial peace that focal points of contact should be eliminated as far as possible'. This, I believe, brings us very near to the heart of the matter, for while the question of race relationships is bound up with many economic, political and administrative issues at heart it is a human question. The claim that those of various ethnic groups can only live peacefully in the same land if they go their separate way in isolation from one another because of their differences of language, culture and colour is a flat denial of both the witness of the Bible and the agelong practice of the Church. One of the most important lessons God has set us to learn in this world is that of learning to live together. In the noisy speeches that are made in favour of *apartheid* far too little attention is paid to the fact that all racial problems are human problems, and this not only in the sense that they relate to the needs of human beings, but also that they must be solved by human beings. Let us face the fact that it is God who has set us all in this land, whatever may be our ethnic group, cultural background and language, so that we may learn to live together. That we can never do if we meet merely in a servant-master relationship and for the rest are content to go our own ways. If we ever had any doubt about this, such doubts ought to have been removed by the attempt that has been made deliberately and systematically during these last years to accomplish this very thing. These last years have seen the rise of racial animosity, the great increase of crime and violence among the African urban population and the growth of political discontent among large sections of the peoples of the Union. Much is heard in these days of the necessity for preserving Western civilization in our land. Let us not forget that any civilization is bound to inspire all who come in contact with it with an urge to independence, an ambition to learn, and a passion for human dignity. Such inspiration cannot be kept from the African peoples. As human beings exposed to the influence of civilization they are bound to go on struggling to secure those things which are due to them because of their value as human beings in the sight of God.

EUROPEANS ARE AFFECTED

But grievous as have been the results of the policies of these last years upon the non-Europeans I am even more perturbed by the effects of such policies upon many white people. There has been, I believe, a noticeable loss in integrity among many

Europeans in recent times. This shows itself in many ways: in a growth in drunkenness and loose living; in the increasing breakdown of family life; in a general deterioration in standards of conduct. It would be an exaggeration to link all this too closely with the policy of compulsory segregation, but I am persuaded that there is some connection between them. History has many examples to show of the evil effects upon a ruling class which has been determined at all cost to retain all the power in its own hands. Too little attention is being paid to the effect that the policies which are now being implemented are having upon the character and moral fibre of the white people in this land.

CHRISTIANITY OR FEAR?

All this suggests that, whatever may be our racial origin, we who claim membership in the body of Christ should lay aside our prejudices and our fears, and search the Scriptures diligently on these matters, and then pray God that He will give us the courage to stand firmly by that which the Bible discloses to us. I say 'pray for courage' advisedly, for one of the most ominous signs of the present situation is the fear that is being created in the hearts and minds of so many people.

The Bishop concluded by speaking of Christian courage; of the need to demonstrate the transforming grace of God in the personal relationships of men and women of different races within the Church.

1956

THE CHURCH IS UNITED IN THE BODY OF CHRIST

WHATEVER may be our differences of colour, culture and class, the unity that is ours in Christ is given visible expression at every Synod. Here we all gather around the one Altar, here we all share in shaping the policy of the Church in this diocese here we all take part in making provision for carrying on the work of the Church during the coming year. At this time year by year we are specially conscious of our unity in Christ, and are made aware afresh that we are members of this new race of human beings which is made up of all those of every ethnic group who have been added to Christ. We are members of that Kingdom in which all human antagonisms are transcended. Yet we shall not interpret aright this unity which is ours in Christ Jesus unless we continually remind ourselves that it has its origin in His death and resurrection. The Church springs out of the deeds of Jesus done in the flesh, and we can only fulfil our destiny in the church as we learn that we are utterly dependent upon the whole Body of Christ. That is equally true for each individual and for each local congregation. Only thus can the Church die to self-sufficiency and self-satisfaction. We are all dependent upon one another, whatever may be our racial origin. Whatever gifts we possess belongs to the Body, and are useful only as they are used in the common life of the Church. All this is made very plain in the New Testament Epistles for in them we are taught that in each local Christian community is a fellowship in which every member is to live in humility and in love to the brethren. Yet no local church is to live to itself. Again and again local churches are reminded of their close relationship to one another, in life, work, worship, pain and death. Not that such a relationship is to be regarded either as a matter of convenience or as a question of organization. On the contrary, this intimate relationship is seen as the direct outcome of the saving work of Christ. This unity with one another, and of local churches with each other, is the unity which belongs to the Body of Christ, arising from the unity of God Himself, uttered in the dying and rising again of Jesus, and now expressed in the order and structure of the Church. All this means that the primary truth about our church membership is not that we are members of a particular congregation, but that we have been born into this new race of human beings, the Christian race, which is made up of people out of every nation and tribe and class. Further, each local church is a church only in so far as it is the expression in a particular place of this new race that has come into the world through Jesus Christ. It is the mighty acts of God in Christ that are the guarantee of our fellowship in the Church.

They alone, made available by the Holy Spirit, can achieve this fellowship in us. 'If God so loved us, we ought also to love one another.' The same mind has to be in us which was also in Christ Jesus. The whole trend of our desires has to be redirected and our whole outlook has to be reorientated if this unity in Christ which we have been considering is to be truly expressed in the life of the Church. In short, it means genuine conversion, a moral revolution.

ARE YOU AFRAID TO BE A CHRISTIAN?

And this unity that is ours in our Lord, this membership in the Body of Christ, this fellowship of the Holy Spirit has to be lived out by us in the ordinary relationships of daily life. Our membership in the Church is something more and other than a sectional interest with which we fill part of our leisure time. It is a way of life and not a pious hobby. The ground of our fellowship with one another in Christ is supernatural, but it has to be manifested in our ordinary daily life. We are to go out into the world carrying in ourselves the final answer to men's problems because Christ Jesus has already won the victory. The everlasting doors have been lifted up and the King of Glory has gone in. Yet we know from our frequent failure that it is never easy to live in His victory. Many of us may find it particularly difficult to do so at the present time. That is not to be wondered at for all around us there are masses of people who are enslaved by all kinds of fear; they are afraid of what those in authority may do to them next; they are afraid of one another; they are afraid of what the future may hold for their children. If this is not sufficient to unnerve them, there are two other disquieting factors in our present situation which must cause all thoughtful people serious concern. In the first place, there is the steadily mounting record of persons convicted of serious crime. Figures for 1953 show that 10 per cent. of our African and Coloured people, 7 per cent. of Asiatics and 6 per cent. of White people were convicted for some offence during that year. It has to be recognized that many Africans are convicted for offences against the pass-laws and other racial legislation. Yet even when allowance has been made for this type of offence it is alarming that the prison population grows larger year by year. Secondly, there is a noticeable deterioration in the general standards of conduct in every section of the population, which shows itself in the increasing disregard for the sacredness of human life as seen in the prevalence of brutal assaults. But it doesn't stop there. It is seen right through our relationships with one another down to the level of rudeness and lack of courtesy. Too many White people appear to be acquiescing in a lowering of their own standards of behaviour. Not that this ought to surprise us for, whenever any dominant group in a community persists in dealing unjustly with those of other groups in society, the standards of the dominant group are always impaired and their moral character impoverished. There are signs that this is already happening among us, and that is perhaps the most disquieting single feature of the contemporary situation.

OUR SOCIETY TODAY IS DISEASED

Unquestionably there are many factors which no doubt contribute to the present diseased condition of our society. At the same time I am persuaded that the conscious and deliberate pursuit of a racialist mythology by those in power among us has to bear a large measure of responsibility for much that is so dark and disturbing in our contemporary scene. As the years pass we are witnessing a steady and mounting elimination of individual rights and their substitution of arbitrary collective standards. Racial prejudices are increasingly being given legal sanctions. Those in authority grow more and more intolerant of any criticism, and tend more and more to exalt the State over the citizen. We see this particularly in much of the type of legislation which continues to pour in a never-ending stream from Parliament. We have only to recall such measures as the Native Areas Consolidation Act and the Natives 'Prohibition of Interdicts' Act, both passed in the last parliamentary session, to realize the force of this contention. The former gives to local authorities wide powers to banish Africans from towns without giving them either any rights to state their cases or any opportunity of appeal against such an order. The latter denies to Africans the right to appeal to the courts against a removal order issued by the Minister until the removal has been completed. These two measures are some indication both of the indifference of those in authority to the rights of the urban Africans, and of their determination to implement their racialist ideology whatever may be the cost in human suffering and frustration.

EDUCATION BY REGULATION

But perhaps we see all this more clearly if we examine what is happening in the field of African education. Eighteen months have passed since the Bantu Education Act became law. As the months pass it is becoming more clear how grave an error it was to pass such an Act devoid of any details. This means that for its working recourse has to be made to a constant stream of regulations. The result is that thousands of African teachers are living in a state of great uncertainty. Not only are they liable to be dismissed or moved with the utmost ease. They are also disturbed, because they believe that some of the members of the new school boards and committees are incompetent to exercise direction in school affairs. Yet serious as these things are, much more serious is the fact that with the pegging of the amount payable out of general revenue for African education at six and a half million pounds, any increase in educational facilities must be paid for by additional African taxation. It is suggested that at the moment the African peoples contribute an insignificant amount to the expenses of government, overlooking entirely the fact that our industries, including farming, are only kept going by the work of the masses of underpaid African workers who thus make a vast contribution to the wealth of the community by their labour, as indeed they do through the millions they contribute to the national revenue through indirect taxation. In any case, in no other civilized country in the world are the poor expected to pay for their own social services. More serious still is the lowering of the minimum education required for teachers to Standard VI plus a three-year course of training. Until the passing of the Bantu Education Act strenuous efforts had been made to increase the professional qualifications of African teachers. Now all this is dismissed as an expensive luxury. Again, any person concerned with the welfare of African children must be gravely disturbed by the doubling of the roll in the sub-standards, and by the introduction of a third compulsory language which may yet prove to be the most serious blow aimed at African education, for, with only half the time available formerly for the study of one of the official languages, the chances of Africans being able to proceed to higher education become increasingly remote.

WHEN IS A UNIVERSITY NOT A UNIVERSITY?

One further aspect of African education demands our notice at this time. I refer to the possible threat to the academic freedom of our universities by the proposal to forbid the Universities of Capetown and the Witwatersrand to continue to admit as students those of all racial groups in South Africa. Just because the object of any university that is worthy of the name must be the pursuit of advancement of knowledge, the only valid criterion for the admission or rejection to its membership must be the academic merit and suitability of the applicant. Freedom of admission, irrespective of considerations of class or colour, ought therefore to be jealously maintained. Further, experience in the Union has shown that the segregation of non-Europeans in their own centres of higher learning frequently results in the development of truculence, suspicion and an unwillingness to co-operate with those of other races on the part of those who are educated in such institutions. Until now the two universities at the Cape and in Johannesburg have rendered a signal service to the whole community by making it possible for men and women students of the various ethnic groups in our society to come to know and understand one another. Wantonly to destroy all that has been achieved through the years by much patient effort is a most serious thing. and if carried through will call forth the condemnation of all those throughout the world who care for the integrity of universities and their freedom to order their own affairs.

THE SOPHIATOWN SCHOOL WAS
TOO EFFICIENT

We cannot leave the question of African education without more than a passing reference to the School of Christ the King in Sophiatown. This action will not be forgotten by numbers of our churchpeople in every ethnic group for a very long time to come. It is illuminating to study the thirty-six columns of Hansard devoted to the debate on this matter. From such a study no sufficient reason emerges for closing a school which in twelve short months had achieved such a fine academic record and which had won such a high place in the regard of thousands of African parents in many centres in and around Johannesburg. It is difficult to avoid the conclusion that our fault, if fault it is, was that at the School of Christ the King we did our job too well.

DENIAL OF FREEHOLD RIGHTS IS
IMMORAL

Speaking of Sophiatown must remind us all of the Western Areas Removal Scheme. Whatever may be said of the merits or otherwise of this scheme we do well to remind ourselves that while it is undoubtedly beneficial to many of the tenants in these areas to be removed from the shacks and hovels in backyards to Meadowlands, there remain a great number of people in those parts who occupy decent residences and who have no desire to move elsewhere. Further, we must never forget that while those who own property are given money compensation they are not allowed to obtain freehold rights in the area to which they are moved. Although this denial of freehold rights in exchange for rights taken away from them is legal it nevertheless remains immoral. The commandment ' Thou shalt not steal ' still stands, and this is one of the clearest breaches of this commandment which has ever taken place among us.

AN AFFRONT TO CHRISTIAN CONSCIENCE

Not dissimilar is the fact that within the last few weeks certain areas in the western suburbs of Johannesburg have been defined in terms of the Group Areas Act. From this proclamation it is clear that twenty thousand African, Coloured, Malay and Chinese people will be compulsorily displaced and removed from areas in which they had lived and worked for many years. This will involve the break-up of long established homes, the destruction of social and cultural institutions laboriously built up through the years, and the serious loss of property investments, as well as the probable elimination of more than seven hundred Indian traders with the consequent deprivation of their means of livelihood. There are many occasions on which it is not easy for us to form a very clear judgment of any particular problem because the issues are so confused. Here the harshness and the injustice of this proposal must be apparent to us all. In plain words a tremendous amount of hardship and suffering is going to be inflicted on thousands of law-abiding people for no other reason than that they do not have white skins. This is a most flagrant disregard for human rights and freedom that we have yet witnessed, and a grave affront to the conscience of all Christian people. As Christians we are bound to set ourselves resolutely against such a needless infliction of cruelty and suffering on human beings, for we are committed to belief in the dignity of human persons and are pledged to uphold justice and freedom in human relationships. Certainly we dare not keep silent in the face of such a tyrannical exercise of authority as is here contemplated. Our plain duty is to make an opportunity to put these proposals before all churchpeople, for this is more than a matter of political views; it is a direct challenge to the Christian conscience and ought to be seen as such by all members of the church.

The Bishop concluded his Charge by exposing the 'hollow sham' of apartheid; by confessing that the Church must admit that it too is infected by racial prejudice; and by appealing for effective expression in Church life of the love of each other which Christ commands.

REPENT OF OUR FAILURE AND OUR SIN

In these, as in other ways, we can even now, through repentance, through worship together, and through activity undertaken in common, do much to remove the reproach under which the Church now stands through our failure and our sin. And in so doing we shall enrich tremendously the witness of the Church in the world. God intends His Church to be drawn from every nation under heaven, claiming no privilege for itself that it is not willing should be afforded to all men, committed to reliance on the power of the Holy Spirit, charged to declare the law and the purpose of God, calling all men of each and every racial group to take their place in this holy fellowship, so that they with us 'may be strong to apprehend with all the saints what is the breadth and length and height and depth, and to know the love of Christ which passeth knowledge.' So in God's mercy may we come to love the Church 'even as Christ also loved the Church, and gave himself up for it; that he might . . . present the Church to himself a glorious Church, not having spot or wrinkle or any such thing; but that it should be holy and without blemish.'

1957

This charge is printed entire.

ATOMIC DANGERS

The Christian churches in South Africa, in common with many people outside the churches, are being compelled by events in our country to give increasing attention to the serious effects of the present policy of compulsory segregation, or 'differential development', both upon the life of the community and upon the lives of great numbers of individuals. Although, quite rightly the Church is deeply concerned with affairs here, this ought not to blind us to the fact that in other parts of the world churchpeople are much more concerned with atomic tests, nuclear weapons, and the dangers of war, than they are with racial questions. This is understandable, because in the great centres of population masses of ordinary people are alarmed by the continuance of the tests of nuclear weapons, and are even more deeply disturbed by the probable consequences that would ensue if such weapons were used in any future international conflict. Already the Central Committee of the World Council of Churches has urged governments conducting nuclear weapon tests to 'forgo them at least for a trial period, either together or individually, in the hope that others will do the same, a new confidence be born, and foundations laid for reliable agreement'. We can only hope and pray that the governments concerned will listen to this earnest plea by church leaders. Atomic warfare, bacteriological weapons, and obliteration bombing together may easily involve the end of civilized life over large areas of the world. One atomic scientist has estimated that one air-raid in which hydrogen bombs are used on the densely populated centres of the United States might mean that as many as forty million people would be killed. As serious as the terrible destruction of human life in any future war, appalling as that would be, is the destruction of moral and spiritual values that war always brings with it. Those of us who have lived at close quarters with modern war know only too well that so many of the worst passions in human beings are aroused at such times. Perhaps this could be excused if it could be maintained that modern total warfare accomplished anything of permanent value. Probably this did happen in war in past centuries, but now it is no longer true. The victors are also the victims. As Professor A. Toynbee says in *War and Civilization* : 'this hope is an illusion : for it is only in fairyland that swords cut Gordian knots which cannot be untied by fingers.'

GOD LIBERATES: THE WORLD ENSLAVES

Yet if we are to come to grips with the issues raised by atomic warfare, we must realize that the discovery of nuclear weapons is simply the culmination of a long period in which men and women have regarded their concern with employing, understanding, and controlling the external world as the primary reason for their existence. Important as this particular enterprise undoubtedly is, in its pursuit human beings have too often forgotten that it always has to be undertaken in a society in which persons as persons are continually in collision with one another. This is the basis of all social existence. We are here not only to explore the world, not even to live, but to learn to live together. And that is an essentially different task from exploring the world. The tragedy is that in wrestling with the external world, men have largely forgotten that the real stuff of life consists in the encounter of person with person and have erroneously concluded that the right management of human affairs depends only upon the acquisition of scientific knowledge. Not for one moment would we deprecate the importance of scientific research, but as churchpeople we are bound to assert that other qualities are needed in the traffic of human beings with one another than those that are necessary in order to penetrate the secrets of nature. We are compelled to recognize that in our dealings with one another goodwill and toleration are not enough. In such dealings we need faith, hope and charity, as well as the capacity for suffering and sacrifice. More than that, our generation has to be reminded that we cannot live responsibly in this world and with one another as persons unless we learn to live with God. Take that away and there is nothing to prevent humanity sinking back into the life of the jungle. Today men and women have to be helped to regain that balance of human life which has been upset by their preoccupation with the control of nature. It is here that a particular responsibility is laid upon the Church, for it remains part of its constant task to recall men to God, in order that they may be set free from slavery to the world. The discovery of the H-bomb brings home in a new and startling fashion the utter insecurity of human life. Yet this ought not to daunt us who claim the name of Christians, for we know that God has prepared a kingdom for those who serve Him; a strong city which has salvation for its walls and bulwarks, because it is rooted in eternity. In this faith we can regain our confidence in face of the terrors that threaten us in this atomic age.

RACISM IS A DANGEROUS MYTH

Yet important as it is for us to direct our attention to this issue of nuclear tests, atomic warfare, and the danger of war, we are bound to continue to devote much thought and effort to the question of race relations, not only because they have deteriorated in an alarming fashion in our country in these last years, but also because colour prejudice and racial discrimination together make up the single most urgent question confronting mankind in this generation. Nothing now more easily arouses the prejudices, animosities and fears of great numbers of people than the dangerous myth of racism does. Yet the manner in which the people of the world deal with the so-called 'colour problem' may well be determinative for the peace of the world. So often it is assumed that peace depends upon the relations between East and West, and more specifically upon the relations between the United States and Soviet Russia. But the chances are that peace between the nations of the world is going to depend upon the way in which the White races of the world respond to the increasing demands for rights and freedom that are now being made by the teeming millions of Asia and Africa as much as it does on the relations between the dominant powers in the modern world. This gives a particular significance to events in the Union and, therefore places a very heavy responsibility upon those in every racial group in our country, for while it is true that our situation is only a part of a total world situation, the problem confronts us in South Africa in a particularly acute form. Here those of many languages, diverse cultures, and differing racial origins have been set by God the tremendous task of learning to live together. We must not waver in recognizing that this is our task, even if the disciples of *apartheid* refuse to accept the fact that this is a multi-racial country and are using every effort to destroy its multi-racial character. Certainly we who are members of the Church have not the slightest excuse for failing to recognize that God has called us to learn to live together in South Africa, because He has set us in His Church in order that in Christ Jesus we may learn to understand, appreciate and respect one another. The Church of God knows no national or racial barriers. Whatever may be the colour of our skin, we

B*

are all God's people. We are all the work of His hands. Each one of us is loved and valued by God, whatever may be our racial origin. For us, each one of us, Christ died.

ASSOCIATION IN WORSHIP IS GOD'S WILL

It was this truth that compelled the Bishops of the Church of the Province of South Africa last Eastertide to declare that if the Minister of Native Affairs used the powers conferred on him in the Native Laws Amendment Act to forbid Africans attending any particular church in an urban area, they would have no alternative but to disobey and to instruct their people to ignore his directive. The position then taken has since been made plain to all churchpeople in the pastoral letters read from the pulpits of all Anglican churches on the fourth Sunday after Trinity. Not that ours has been the only voice heard in this matter. Leaders in many churches other than our own have expressed their determination to resist this monstrous encroachment by the State upon the conscience and liberty of human beings to worship together. Naturally we earnestly hope that this particular provision of the Native Laws Amendment Act will never be used against any church. But if it should be so used we are resolutely determined to resist any such attempt. Not that we intend to use this clause as an opportunity to make demonstrations against the powers now taken by the secular authorities. At the same time we are resolved to continue our present practice, and to encourage our people in every way possible in the task of building up churchpeople of different racial origin into that unity in Christ in His Church which God has called us to achieve in the household of faith.

THE CHURCH'S CARE FOR EVERY MAN

In directing attention especially to the so-called 'church clause' in the Native Laws Amendment Act we are fully aware that there is much else in other legislation which ought to concern us as churchpeople. It is true that this particular issue directly concerns the inner life of the churches as churches, but if the Church is to be faithful to its calling it ought never to restrict its attention to those matters which directly concern its own life. As members of the Church we are compelled to be concerned with anything that affects the well-being of our fellow-members in racial groups other than our own. Indeed our concern ought not to end even there, for while the primary function of the Church is to be the People of God, we are also set in the world to win the world for Christ. The Church, therefore, must be concerned with all that affects the life of all human beings in the community, even if at the moment they remain outside our borders as a church. Unfortunately, as we look back over the months since we last met in Synod, much legislation has been enacted which has been based upon discrimination against one or other racial group in the community, and which is leading to much suffering, frustration and resentment for many of the inhabitants of South Africa.

AN INEQUITABLE ACT

A glaring example of this is the method by which the Group Areas Act, as amended on various occasions, is now being implemented in various parts of the Union. From what is happening it is becoming clear that under this Act Indians are going to be deprived of the legitimate results of their industry. Some Africans are going to lose the meagre freehold rights that they have so far enjoyed in certain urban areas, and far larger numbers of them who are an integral part of our town and city communities are going to be denied any possibility of stable property rights. Those who care for the well-being and stability of our social life cannot help viewing with the gravest concern the consequences that the application of the Group Areas Act is having, and is going to have, for a large section of the inhabitants of our country. In Johannesburg the shape of things to come becomes clearer each month. Here nine thousand Indians are to be removed and between seven and eight hundred Indian traders are to be uprooted from areas in which through many years they have built up profitable businesses. Apparently the authorities consider that the Indians in our community have committed some crime in having devoted their lives to the building up of private enterprise.

Indeed, the treatment given them is so cruel that it seems as if the intention is to drive them to seek expatriation. Still it is not only Africans and Indians who will suffer grievously by the implementation of the Group Areas Act. The Coloured people will also be exposed to much hardship and loss. Something of what this will mean can be clearly seen by looking at the threat to Albertsville. This is an area which for many years has been exclusively owned and occupied by Coloured people. Because those in authority have decided that this well-ordered and attractive suburb must become an area for White occupation, four thousand people must be uprooted and compelled against their wills to live elsewhere. Grave as have been the injustices that have been committed in these last years in the endeavour to place the whole population of South Africa in the strait-jacket of compulsory segregation, few things that have yet happened have been so iniquitous as that which is now taking shape through the implementation of the Group Areas Act.

PASS CARRYING *AD NAUSEAM*

Another matter which is causing increasing concern at the present time is the attempt that is being made to extend the system of pass laws to African women. This is being done at a time when an increasing number of Africans regard the pass laws which govern the employment, residence and movement of male Africans, as being amongst the most notorious of the discriminatory legislation under which they suffer. Further, account has to be taken of the fact that these laws are working very badly among the male African population as can be seen from the large and ever increasing numbers of African men who are imprisoned each year for some offence against these laws. All this suggests that the attempt now being made to extend these laws to African women is the height of folly, especially when it is remembered that there is a deep, widespread hostility among African people to any extension of the pass system in whatever form for their womenfolk.

AN IMPOSSIBLE BURDEN

One serious consequence of all this discriminatory legislation is the almost impossible burden that is being placed upon those on whom the responsibility rests for the maintenance of law and order. Yet the fact that this is so in no way excuses the conduct of some of the members of the police force on more than one occasion. Indeed, few things are more disturbing than irresponsible behaviour by those who are charged to be guardians of the law. To say that is in no sense either to minimize the difficulties of their task, or to deny that the behaviour of many members of the police force at all times is exemplary. While recognizing this, however, I am compelled to recall that at the time of the disturbance outside the treason trial I had occasion to draw attention to the severe handling of the crowd by some members of the police force. This might be dismissed as of small importance if it was an isolated incident, were it not that there was similar provocative action on the part of some members of the police force during the bus boycott. Further, from statements made to me after troubles at Evaton and Newclare, and more recently in the Western Transvaal and Orlando, it is difficult to avoid the conclusion that the actions of some of the police on such occasions cannot be justified.

As I said last December, one cannot help feeling sorry for young and inexperienced policemen who so often find themselves in situations with which they are so ill-equipped to deal. But this fact does not excuse unrestrained behaviour on their part, still less the unprovoked attacks that are made from time to time on members of the public. The Church cannot stand by silent when such things are happening. We are bound to express serious disquiet at many of the reports which reach us, for in so doing we not only wish to draw the attention of those in authority to evils which ought to be remedied, but also desire to strengthen the hands of the many in the police force itself who are anxious to maintain high standards of conduct among those who are entrusted with the maintenance of law and order in our land.

COLOUR VALUES

Important as it is for the Church to examine events from the standpoint of the Christian conscience, it is even more important that the dogma that lies behind the policies now being implemented in our country should be carefully scrutinized both in the light of Christian ethics and the Biblical doctrine of the Church. At first sight this is a difficult task because, quite understandably, many people are confused by the fact that this idea of *apartheid* is now used in so many different senses by different people, ranging from the idealistic form of the total separation of every ethnic group from each other to unblushing White domination. Indeed, recently the concept of *apartheid* has been further confused by the use of the phrase 'practical *apartheid*', by which is presumably meant some modification of present policies to take account of the realities of our situation. Yet we ought not to be as confused as we often are, because however varied may be the senses in which this word *apartheid* is used, the assumptions which lie behind its use are always the same. Two assumptions are always made. First it is assumed that it is impossible for us to learn to live together in South Africa. The fact, beyond all argument, that Black, White, Coloured, and Indian are all inhabitants of South Africa apparently has no significance at all for the apostles of *apartheid*. On the contrary, they are determined to destroy the multi-racial character of our society whatever may be the cost in doing so. Secondly, it is assumed that the White group is and always will be superior to all other groups in our country, not on grounds either of culture or of religion, but of race. While we may quite rightly deplore discrimination on grounds of religion or culture, to do so on grounds of racial differences is even more serious an error, for it fixes a gulf that is for ever impassable, and has as its criterion the most superficial, trivial, and insignificant aspect of any human being, namely the colour of his skin.

THE GREAT IMMORALITY

But what has the Christian ethic to say of *apartheid*? Can

such a theory, whatever form it may take, ever be justifiably defended upon ethical grounds? Before we can answer such questions accurately we must first remind ourselves that the Christian ethic, while it in no sense ignores the social aspects of human life, emphasizes the value of each individual human being, his worth as a person, and his capacity to respond to other human beings with generosity and sacrifice. The cardinal error of *apartheid* is that it never regards human beings as individuals. It persists in ignoring their personal worth because it always treats them as members of a particular ethnic group, and in so doing personifies the racial group, the tribe, the race. Indeed, it declares in effect that the individual has worth only as he has value to the racial group to which he happens to belong. Such a theory must be condemned as unethical. It is at this point that *apartheid* demonstrates most clearly that it is immoral, because it seeks to deal with people not as persons, but as members of a particular racial group. Further, a study of the legislation which has been passed in order to translate this theory into practice shows that frequently it is compelled to deal unjustly with those who have not white skins. Those who take their stand on the Christian ethic cannot possibly defend a theory which demands so much and such grave injustice for so many people in order to make it effective in the life of the community. This concept of *apartheid*, whatever form it may take, is an evil and a vicious thing, against which the Church has no alternative but to struggle, if it is to be true to the ethic of the New Testament.

GOD THE HOLY SPIRIT MAKES ALL MEN ONE

This becomes even more apparent when we examine the Biblical doctrine of the Church. From the day of Pentecost onwards the hall-mark of the Church has been the fellowship of the Holy Spirit. The Holy Spirit is now possessed by every member of the Body of Christ, without distinction of sex or class or race. Anyone who reads the New Testament writings even cursorily cannot fail to notice that the evidence of the Holy Spirit working in the Church is His capacity to break down the middle wall of partition. St Paul asserts this emphatically, and he can do so with such confidence because he had seen with his own eyes the Holy Spirit working across the boundaries of race and colour. Truly the events at the Council at Jerusalem indicate that the fellowship of the Holy Spirit was only achieved at great cost and with much pain. But the point is that it was achieved by the power of the Holy Spirit. That is a fact of history. And what was accomplished in the Church by the Holy Spirit in the first days has been repeated over and over again in the long history of the Church. Again and again men and women who have redirected their life Christwards, and who have allowed the Holy Spirit to have His way with them, have been enabled to render to one another and to all men their due, irrespective of their race or colour. How different is this fellowship of the Holy Spirit from that form of society which the apostles of *apartheid* would enforce in our country. As members of the Church we may not be able to do a great deal to prevent them from accomplishing their designs, but we can recognize that the form of society they are seeking to fashion bears no resemblance to that fellowship of faith into which God has called us and which God intends to be the pattern for human society. We may be compelled to live in a society shaped according to the dictates of *apartheid*, but that gives us no excuse for accepting it in our hearts. God is showing us some better thing in His Church. To that we must be true.

NO HOPE WITHOUT A CHANGE OF HEART

Thus, when we examine this dogma of *apartheid* in the light of Christian ethics and the Biblical doctrine of the Church, we are driven to two conclusions. In the first place it is flagrantly immoral to attempt to maintain White supremacy in a racially mixed society. Secondly, it is contrary to what God wills for us in this land to attempt to construct a form of society which is so greatly at variance to that which God has disclosed to us in His Church. For these reasons we have no alternative but to demand a radical change immediately in our national policy. Yet, as Professor B. B. Keet pointed out in his recent Hoernlé Memorial Lecture, for this to happen 'the one essential condition is that a change of heart must take place, and the European's approach to this greatest of all problems must be radically altered.' But we may ask, where is such a change to begin? Surely we must begin with ourselves. So we would earnestly appeal to the White members of our Synod, and through them to the whole body of the faithful in our diocese, to do more than recognize that present policies in our land are doomed to failure and are bound to end in destruction. That is certainly the case. But more is asked of us than this. The hour has come when each one of us ought to make the supplication of the psalmist of old our own, and pray to God to put a new and right spirit within us, and in our daily dealings with one another of different racial origin to act upon our prayer. To be effective such a change of heart must come to all of us, and to each one of us personally. No longer must we attempt to satisfy our consciences merely by making pronouncements on racial matters. We must be prepared to take the Christian ethic seriously and give ourselves more zealously than in past days to the task of building up a Church in this land which will more nearly resemble the Church of apostolic days. In short, we have to be ready to take the path of racial co-operation, however costly it may be for us to do so. Not that this appeal is made only to those of European descent in the Church. Our African churchpeople have also to overcome their suspicions and antipathies, realize that they have much still to learn of the requirements of life in a Christian community, and demonstrate that they are willing and able to take responsibility, for only thus can real co-operation be secured among us. Most of all, whatever may be our racial origin, we must show that we are worthy of one another's trust. In our present situation it is imperative that we do all in our power to remove suspicion, create trust, mutual respect and understanding between ourselves. It would be foolish to pretend that all this is going to be easy, for it will mean that in the foreseeable future the chances are that we shall have to struggle against the prevailing opinions in our land. But that ought not to daunt us. It is always creditable to oppose erroneous ideas, however powerful they may be. And in so doing we may find a simple way to follow Christ in bearing the cross. 'Not that we are sufficient of ourselves, to think anything as of ourselves; but our sufficiency is of God.' To this we must cling, for the law and purpose that we seek are God's, and our own, even though we are conscious of how far short we fall of all that God demands of us. Still, we must condemn injustice, oppression and selfish ambition, while at the same time we strive to build up in the Church a better way of life together than the peoples of our land yet know. And, in the midst of all the turmoil and the conflict that surrounds us, let us ever remember that we stand in the succession of them who in this world have no abiding city, for they sought a city which lies beyond the horizon of this world, 'the holy city, new Jerusalem, coming down out of heaven from God. . . . And the city has no need of sun or moon to shine upon it, for the glory of God is its light, and its lamp is the Lamb. By its light shall the nations walk . . . they shall bring glory into it, the glory and the honour of the nations.' To that city may God in his mercy bring us all.

THE LIQUIDATION OF
ADAMS COLLEGE

This account by the Principal, the Rev. G. C. Grant, of the attempt of the College authorities to respond positively to the challenge of the racial policies of the Union Government is presented as a case study in the interaction of the policies of mission-school authorities and of the Government, and to show the circumstances under which Christian leaders have been doing their work. It is a shortened version of a longer report privately printed in the U.S.A.

INTRODUCTION

I N the year 1853 missionaries of the American Board, Boston, founded on the banks of the Amanzimtoti River, Natal, the first school in the Province. In its early days it was called Amanzimtoti Institute, but in recent years it was called Adams College, after the pioneer medical missionary of Natal, Dr. Newton Adams.

Like many another institution, the College grew; and in the process of time it catered for more and more students and provided more and more courses. During the course of its history it has pioneered in a number of ways, notably in its appointing of promising Africans to responsible posts. Chief A. J. Luthuli, for instance, was the first African to be appointed to the staff of a High School, while Professor Z. K. Matthews was the first African to be appointed Principal of a High School with Europeans under him. In like manner, Mr R. Guma was the first African to be appointed Principal of a Teachers' Training College.

Equally important is the fact that in the Constitution of the College provision was made for more and more past students in particular and other interested Africans in general to become members of its Governing Council, and eventually to take full control of the College.

There is no gainsaying the fact that a considerable proportion of the leading Africans of South Africa and adjacent territories have been trained at Adams. It is also true that the College has made an invaluable contribution to the advancement of the status and the welfare of Africans. It is equally true that it is held in high esteem by many people of many races in many lands. Yet this College with its fine record of service and achievement extending over a hundred years has been liquidated. The question that arises is: 'Why has this happened?' The purpose of this report is to help supply the answer to that question.

I

THE BANTU EDUCATION ACT— ITS ORIGIN AND EFFECTS

ON the 19th January, 1949—the very month in which the writer began to be Principal of Adams College—the Government appointed a Commission to inquire into and report upon what it was pleased to call 'Bantu Education'. The terms of reference, however, were heavily weighted in favour of *apartheid*, and the membership included no African, and no member of the missionary churches which had pioneered the field of African education and still had most to do with it. After three years and more of painstaking and intensive work the Commission presented its report. It presented recommendations in keeping with the political desires of the Nationalist Government; and the Government naturally made it known that they approved of the Report, notwithstanding representations made from competent bodies whose views differed. It was no surprise, therefore, when the Government in 1953 brought forward a bill to give legislative effect to the recommendations of the Commissioners. This was called the Bantu Education Bill.

The main purpose of the Bill as stated in the preamble was 'to provide for the transfer of the administration and control of Native Education from the several provincial administrations to the Government of the Union', as well as to transfer the control and administration of Native Education from the Education Department to the Native Affairs Department, and to give the Minister of Native Affairs extensive arbitrary powers over the realm of Bantu Education.

When the contents of the Bill were published, the writer and his wife took every opportunity available to write and speak against the objectionable sections, particularly against the arbitrary powers given to the Minister. Our criticisms were levelled not only at the administrative paraphernalia but at the principle, the purpose, and the assumptions of the Bill.

Though the official Opposition in Parliament fought the Bill valiantly their efforts were of no avail. The Government majority saw to it that the Bill became law, and what was once the Bantu Education Bill became the Bantu Education Act.

As always, the Nationalist Government was sensitive to criticism, all the more so as it came from one whom they could dub 'un-South African'. Consequently as a result of our opposition to the Bill—at least, that is our reading of the situation—the Government swiftly took its revenge. Early in 1954, just as the new school year was about to begin, five C.I.D. representatives turned up at the College armed with a warrant to search my office and home. Hereunder is a copy of the Search Warrant:

SEARCH WARRANT

ISSUED IN TERMS OF SECTION 49 OF ACT 31/1917, AS AMENDED

To all Police officers

WHEREAS it appears to me from information taken on oath that the following goods, viz:
LODGERS (sic), CASH BOOKS, DAY BOOKS, ACCOUNT BOOKS, INVOICES, CHEQUE BOOKS, DEPOSIT SLIPS, BANK STATEMENTS,

FINANCIAL RETURNS, CIRCULARS, CIRCULAR INSTRUCTIONS, LETTERS OF INSTRUCTIONS, BOOKS OF ACCOUNT, MINUTE BOOKS, PAMPHLETS, DRAFT SPEECHES, PLANS OF CAMPAIGN, NOMINAL ROLLS, LETTERS, TELEGRAMS, CABLEGRAMS, DIARIES, and any other correspondence, the property or in the lawful possession of one G. C. GRANT, Principal, Adams College, Adams Mission, Umbumbulu,

being anything as to which there are reasonable grounds for believing that it will afford evidence as to the commission of any offence, to wit (a) Treason (b) Sedition (c) Conspiracy (d) Act 44 of 1950 (e) Act 27 of 1914 (f) Act 8 of 1953, are concealed in, upon or about the dwelling house, or in, upon or about the Administrative offices of the said College situated at Adams Mission, Umbumbulu in the occupation of G. C. GRANT.

THESE are therefore in HER MAJESTY'S name, to authorize and require you, with necessary and proper assistance, to enter the said dwelling house or Administrative Offices in the day time, and there diligently to search for the said goods; and if the same or any part thereof, shall be found on such search, that you bring the goods so found before the Magistrate at Umbumbulu to be disposed of and dealt with according to law.

Given under my hand at Durban this 22nd day of January, 1954.

(Signed) M. C. Lamprecht, Capt.
JUSTICE OF THE PEACE, NATAL.

The men assigned to this unpleasant task were courteous in the discharge of their duties. One who was searching through my personal letters stopped when he came across a letter from the Natal Cricket Association and said, ' I see that you play cricket.' Apparently he was unaware of the fact that in days gone by I was an international cricketer. A little later his eyes fastened on another letter. This time it was one in which I offered to the College Council the sum of £5,000 as a gift from my wife and me towards the Centenary Appeal. When he had perused this letter he had the decency to make the remainder of his search perfunctory. In telling this story to my friends I always take delight in the fact that before the men left they accepted my wife's invitation to have a cup of tea; while I always kick myself for forgetting to get them to sign our Visitors' Book.

Before leaving this incident I should add that following the visit of the C.I.D. Officers representations through private channels were made to the Minister of Justice against its injustice, and the only answer received was that on the information provided to the police they had no option to take the steps which they did. In other words, Adams College in general and its Principal in particular were marked down for special attention. The struggle for survival had begun.

II

THE BANTU EDUCATION ACT IN OPERATION

IN accordance with the provisions of the Bantu Education Act a new department called the Bantu Education Department under the Native Affairs Department was established as from 1st January, 1954. The officer appointed to the head of this new department was Mr F. J. de Villiers, a man with considerable experience in African Education. What is of special interest is that Mr de Villiers in his early teaching days had been a teacher at Adams, and equally interesting is the fact that only a few months before I came to Adams he had been offered the Principalship of the College. There were thus those who expected much from him. I, on the other hand, could not share these high hopes. Indeed, instead of writing and congratulating Mr de Villiers on his appointment, I wrote and told him where I stood—namely, that I was opposed to the very things which he was called upon to encourage. As far as I could judge he bore me no ill will for my frank expression of opinion.

One of Mr de Villiers' first tasks as Under-Secretary for Bantu Education was to tour the country in what he called 'an exploratory capacity', and meet those most closely concerned with Bantu Education. During the course of these exploratory tours he did his best to 'sell' the advantages of the new administrative machinery with its centralization and to call for the fullest co-operation. He even asked that if the members of his audience had any suggestions to make or any matters requiring attention they could present these to him in the form of a Memorandum. Taking him at his word, I went to great pains to prepare such a memorandum about the College, and with the approval of the College Council I presented it to him. Not even an acknowledgment has been made of it.

Just at this juncture, I am sorry to say, I had good reason to believe that the services of a senior member of staff should be terminated. Let us call him 'Mr A'. I reported my findings to my Governing Council, which took the necessary steps to terminate his services. The immediate outcome was the receipt in quick succession of two telegrams. The first was from the Regional Director of Bantu Education, Natal, saying: 'Strongly recommend retention "Mr A" until December in best interests of peace at Adams.' The second was from the Secretary for Native Affairs and read: 'Department very much concerned regarding action Governing Council in terminating "Mr A's" services. Secretary Native Affairs requests that "Mr A" be retained until decision is taken regarding future status of Adams College.'

This concern on the part of the Government showed that even at this early stage the future status of the College was under their consideration. This concern was also none other than a veiled threat to our continued existence, particularly to our existence as an independent institution. Happily, our Governing Council stood firm, refused to reinstate 'Mr A', and replied that it had done what, in its considered judgment, it felt satisfied was in the best interests of peace and harmony at Adams. Thus ended Round One.

The next round began in August, 1954, with the issue by this new Bantu Education Department of two important Circulars concerning the future of all Bantu educational institutions. The first dealt exclusively with 'The Transfer of control of Teacher Training Schools to the State', and the second with 'The Transfer of State-Aided Schools to Bantu Community Organizations, except in the case of Teacher Training Schools'.

As far as Teacher Training was concerned the Government

made it perfectly clear that in future all teacher training would be done by the State and by the State only. Mission institutions with Teacher Training departments had no alternative but to hand them over to the Government or to cease operating them. They could, however, if they wished, continue to run the boarding establishments. The only choice therefore open to the Missions was to close their Training Colleges *in toto* or in part.

As far as educational activities other than Teacher Training was concerned the Government gave a choice. Perhaps choice is hardly the appropriate word. Nevertheless, an opportunity was given to those who cared to do so to continue their work provided they supplied all the funds. It was pointed out that all *per capita* grants would cease altogether, while the subsidies for teachers' salaries would be progressively reduced by as much as 25% in the first year, and by an equal amount in the following three years. In other words, in four years such schools as desired to do what they had previously been doing would be without any Government subsidy at all.

In the face of such unilateral action on the part of the Government the reaction of those most concerned varied considerably. These may be divided into five main groups.

The first group consisted of those who welcomed with relief the release from the worry and financial burden of their educational work. Among these were those who felt that they could now concentrate more fully and effectively on their primary work of evangelism.

The second group were those who disliked the new proposals but could not face the financial consequences which continuance of their educational work without subsidy would entail. Consequently they accepted the conditions with the intention of making the best of a bad bargain. In this group were to be found many Methodists, many Bishops of the Anglican Communion, and many another. This was easily the largest section.

The third group consisted of the Roman Catholic Church, which while prepared to co-operate with the Government as far as possible was at the same time determined at all costs to maintain its primary schools at least. In fact, the Roman Catholic Church launched a most successful campaign to secure the funds required for this work.

The fourth group was small, and comprised those like Bishop Reeves of Johannesburg and Father Huddleston of the Community of the Resurrection, who roundly proclaimed that the new proposals were evil, so evil that they would have nothing to do with them. Rather than lease, rent or sell their buildings they would close them—and this they did.

The fifth group was the smallest of all, and consisted of only three institutions known to the writer. One of these three was Adams College. The answer of Adams College can be divided into two parts. As far as Teacher Training was concerned, the College regretted the decision of the Minister to take out of its hands the training of teachers, and stated that it had no option but to abide by that decision. The College expressed itself anxious, however, that this decision should not interrupt the flow of trained teachers. The College was, therefore, willing and offered to continue to carry on a Teacher Training College for a further period of years until such time as the Government could make adequate alternative arrangements. At the same time, the College considered it impossible for a Training College to be established and run on the College premises by a separate authority. Therefore it was not in a position to rent, sell, or lease to the Department buildings or other amenities for the purpose of a Training College separately run and controlled.

As far as our High and Industrial Schools were concerned, the College regretted the decision of the Minister to reduce subsidies hitherto paid, asserted that it had neither the desire nor the power in terms of its constitution to abandon the work for which it was formed, and declared that the College would, therefore, continue, so long as it was able to do so, to carry on its High and Industrial Schools as institutions under its own control with such subsidy as the Government was willing to offer.

This decision deserves attention. In the first place, it showed that the College was prepared to accept the challenge of the Government and run what it could for as long as it could. Secondly, it showed that the College was prepared to make a venture of faith, as it was unendowed and at the same time alive to the financial implications of such a venture. Thirdly, it showed that while the College was prepared to stand up for its rights it was not prepared to break the law or refuse

Government assistance. 'So long as it is able to do so'—these are the key words.

Our letter to the Government conveying our decision was duly acknowledged, but our offer to continue to run our Teacher Training College until adequate alternative arrangements could be made was turned down on the grounds that they 'would be able to make the necessary provision to maintain the flow of trained teachers without taking advantage of this offer'. Thus ended the second round of our struggle for survival.

During this period of decision we were immensely helped by two events.

The first event was that the American Board of Commissioners for Foreign Missions, Boston—whose missionaries had founded the College and whose officers still had a deep concern for its welfare—cabled that they were prepared to provide over and above their then annual contribution in men and money a further annual grant of $10,000. Secondly, we learnt with much joy that the British Council of Churches had requested Mr L. Bruce Greaves, O.B.E., and the Rev. W. Fenton Morley to visit South Africa to make personal contact with church leaders, and to report back within six weeks. It was the knowledge that responsible Christian bodies overseas were ready to help that encouraged us to persevere in our stand.

It was on this note of achievement and confidence that 1954 ended.

III

THE GATHERING STORM

THE year 1955 began quietly, but it was but the calm before the storm. Hardly had the new school year began than we received a letter from the Under-Secretary, Mr. F. J. de Villiers, calling upon the College 'to reconsider its decision and explore the alternative course whereby the full subsidy may continue to be paid, a course which will have to be followed sooner or later'. A few months earlier we had been presented with harsh alternatives. We had accepted the challenge of the harsh alternative. Now we were told that even this harsh alternative could not be ours. Sooner or later, we were reminded, we should be put out of action. So much for the Government's declaration that a choice was available to those who ventured to run a private school.

On 1st June the following letter from the Secretary for Native Affairs was received:

> SECRETARY FOR NATIVE AFFAIRS
> MARKS BUILDING,
> CAPE TOWN
> 26th May, 1955

The Principal
Adams College
P.O. Adams Miss. St.
Natal

Dear Sir,

With further reference to your letter of 28th February, 1955, concerning the future of Adams College, I am directed to enquire whether your Council is aware of the fact that its proposals in this regard do not reflect the desires of the Bantu residents of the Umlazi district.

A statement received from our Regional Bantu Education Office, Pietermaritzburg, reads as follows:

> 'On January 14th, 1955, a full meeting of the Chiefs and headmen of the Umlazi Magistracy passed a unanimous resolution condemning the action of the Adams Council in closing down the Adams Training College. The meeting requested both the Native Commissioner and the Inspector of Schools to pass this resolution on to the higher authority.
> The points made by the chiefs who spoke were:
>
> (1) That Adams and the Glebe upon which it stands were held in trust for the Native people and could not be regarded as private property belonging to the Adams Council or the American Board.
> (2) That much of the money that went to build and maintain Adams came from the Native people and the money contributed by the Government, the American

Board Mission and the general public was for the purpose of advancing the Native. That much of this money had been given specifically for Teacher-Training.

(3) That such property could not be used as the Adams Council thought fit because it disagreed with Governmental policy. The Native people should have been fully consulted.

(4) That the meeting of Chiefs and headmen demanded the restoration of the Training College as soon as possible.'

The attitude adopted by this meeting of Bantu leaders appears to be entirely reasonable and cannot be ignored.

The Department was, as you know, prepared to consider proposals in regard to the conversion of Adams into a Departmental institution, with full control of the existing schools and hostels, subject to mutually satisfactory financial arrangements.

I am now directed to inform you that the Minister wishes you to know that he is still prepared to consider such proposals but that in the existing circumstances, he is no longer prepared to authorize subsidy payments to Adams College, as at present constituted, after December, 1955.

Should it still be your aim 'to run the two schools as entirely private schools', notwithstanding the attitude of the Bantu community and notwithstanding the desire of the Department to use this institution for teacher-training, you are, in accordance with the regulations, entitled to apply for their registration as such. This should be done at your earliest convenience and not later than 20th June.

If such an application is received the Honourable the Minister of Native Affairs will consider your application and you will, in due course, be advised in regard to the outcome. Applications in this connection are governed by paragraph 9, subsection (e) of the Bantu Education Act. See also the Bantu Educational Journal, February, 1955, page 69, section 3 (b).

Yours faithfully,
(Signed) W. W. M. EISELEN,
Secretary for Native Affairs.

To this we replied:

The Secretary
Native Affairs   21st June, 1955
P.O. Box 384
PRETORIA

Dear Sir,

Your letter No. 44/302 of the 26th May, addressed to the Principal was received by him on the 1st inst, and carefully considered by the Council of Governors of the College at its last meeting.

I have been instructed to advise you that the Council notes with regret that the Minister is no longer prepared to authorize subsidy payments to Adams College after December, 1955. As the time allowed to the College to make application for registration expires in terms of your letter on the 20th inst, the Council has, in the meantime, decided to make such application without waiting for a reply to this letter and the application has already been transmitted to you. It would be appreciated if that application could be considered and decided at an early date irrespective of any consideration of the points raised in this letter.

I have further been instructed by my Council to assure you that the decisions that the College has taken in regard to its future have not been taken because the College has the desire to challenge Government policy. The College has an honest and sincere belief—even if the belief is mistaken—that, if it continues to carry on its schools, it can make a contribution for the benefit of the Bantu people. The Council also wishes me to assure you that your letter was the first intimation that it has ever had that it was definitely desired by the Department to use the College for Teacher Training.

When Messrs Prozesky and Jensen of your Department met the Council of Governors to discuss the future of the Training College, they were at considerable pains to explain that, even if the Council were to accept the alternative offered to it of handing over the Training College to the Department instead of the alternative of having it closed down, there was no certainty that the Department would accept the offer. In fact they went so far as to say to the members of the Council that it would be a struggle to persuade the Department to continue a Teachers' Training College there, as the Teachers' Training College buildings were totally inadequate for the purpose for which they were then being used. You will also no doubt recollect that when the College communicated its decision to you, it did offer to continue to run the Training College until such time as the Department was in a position to provide other alternative accommodation for the students, but that offer was refused.

With respect it would appear that the College's peculiar position has been overlooked by the Department. The College is a non-profit company registered under the Companies Act, 1926, with a constitution by which it is in law bound and from which it is not entitled to depart. That Constitution binds it to carry on 'Adams College' as such in perpetuity or to return the property that it received, that is to say all the land and buildings erected thereon, to the American Board of Commissioners for Foreign Missions. The College is not in itself a Missionary Institution in the true sense of that term, though it has a history and a tradition as well as a constitution that binds it to follow certain Missionary principles.

In this connection I ought to add and perhaps to emphasize that many of the members of the Company are members of the Bantu race and that the decisions taken by the College were taken at general meetings of the Company at which the large majority of those present were members of that race. The Members of the College consist of past students (these include parents of some of the College's students), past and present members of the Staff who have served the College for a specific number of years and who have taken the trouble to apply for membership of the Company, a limited number of representatives of the American Board Mission and persons who, having donated to College funds, apply for membership of the Company. In these circumstances the College feels that it has, so far as it is, in law, entitled to do so, taken into account the views of, and consulted with the Bantu people interested in the College.

I am furthermore instructed to advise you that your letter was the first intimation that the Council of Governors had of any meeting of the Chiefs and Headmen of the Umlazi

Magistracy at which the College was discussed. Without wishing to discuss at length the points made by those who spoke at the meeting, the Council feels that it is unfortunate that it was not given an opportunity of being present on that occasion to discuss the matter with them. Suffice it to say that the Council can assure you in all honesty and without any desire to be controversial that the statements made at that meeting are not in accord with facts.

In all the circumstances therefore, my Council asks that the Honourable the Minister be good enough to reconsider his decision to withdraw the subsidy payments to Adams College as from 31st December next.

Finally, I am requested to ask you exactly what the Department requires of Adams College Incorporated bearing in mind its legal inability to hand over its schools as such whether they be the Training School, the High School or the Industrial School to any other controlling authority except to return the schools to the American Board Mission. Perhaps the Minister would be prepared to consider deeming the members of the Incorporated Company to be a Bantu Community Organization for the purpose of the Act.

Yours faithfully,
(Signed) J. V. HOSKEN,
Secretary.

A letter from an African friend, whose name and address I cannot disclose for fear of the consequences to him, gives a much more vigorous retort.

My dear Mr Grant,

Thank you very much for your letter dated 7.6.55 containing a copy of a letter from the Secretary for Native Affairs. I have just read it 2 minutes ago and I am putting down the thoughts which have passed through my mind as I was reading it. These thoughts may not be very sound: they may even be stupid. Anyhow here they are:

1. I attach no importance whatever to the statement or argument that the proposals of the Council do not reflect the desires of the Bantu residents of the Umlazi district—first, because the residents do not know the

views of the Council. The Chiefs and Headmen had no justification, therefore, for condemning the action of the Adams College Council before they heard its views.

2. The Chiefs and Headmen know hardly anything about the implications of the Bantu Education Act except what they were told by the officers who are responsible for interpreting the Act to them.

3. The Adams College Council was not represented at the meeting of Chiefs, etc., where its action was condemned. And why was Adams College discussed at a meeting of which the Council was not aware?

4. The Secretary for Native Affairs does not indicate the manner in which the Native people of the Umlazi District could have been consulted by the College Council, and it is difficult to understand how the Council could be penalized for this when the Department itself (or the Government for that matter) did not consult the Native people before it introduced and passed the Bantu Education Act. The Department is not justified in upholding a demand for full consultation with the Native people whom it *does not consult* on any legislation which affects them. I am almost certain that the very same Chiefs and Headmen would not have supported the Minister of Native Affairs if he had consulted them *before* he introduced the Bill (Bantu Education Act) in Parliament.

If the Secretary for Native Affairs is sincere he should arrange for a meeting where the Chiefs and Headmen could hear the views of the Adams College Council.

5. Can the Secretary for Native Affairs say that the Native Chiefs, etc., who spoke at that unfortunate meeting of January 15th, 1955, were themselves expressing the views of the African people in the Umlazi district? Had they obtained their views before they went to that meeting or were they just expressing their views as individuals?

Yours sincerely,

Arising out of this letter, I sent invitations to the Chiefs and Headmen of the Umlazi Magistracy to come to the College

C

and discuss with me matters affecting the College. After one postponement, about ten of them came—that is, about three-fifths of the number invited. For the most part they were unsophisticated, uneducated, simple men, who were not alive to the issues involved. In the words of Professor Z. K. Matthews and Dr D. G. S. M'timkhulu: 'although these men as a body with few exceptions represent the most unenlightened section of the African population they are regarded by the Government as the real leaders of thought among Africans.'

With the aid of an interpreter I spoke to them and answered their questions for some two and a half hours. I explained to them what decision the College had taken and why. I made every effort to disabuse their minds of the idea that it was the College authorities who had closed the Teacher Training College; and I tried equally hard to get them to understand that the responsibility for the closing rested squarely on the shoulders of the Government. To my delight they inquired what they could do to mend matters. Not to embarrass them with the powers that be, I advised them to do nothing there and then, but I urged them that should matters concerning the College crop up in any of their future meetings, they should ask that a representative of the College be invited to speak on behalf of the College. This they agreed was likely to be the best procedure.

From my office they came with me to my home and here an extraordinary thing happened. After lunch one of the Chiefs said that he wanted to do something for the College. Thereupon he called on all present to kneel down, and without more ado he prayed for God's blessing upon the College. Shortly after this, they took their departure, leaving behind their best wishes and their assurances that in future they would not pass judgment on any matter affecting the College before they had heard the College's point of view.

In the letter from the Secretary for Native Affairs the College was called upon to submit, if it so desired, its application for Registration as a Private School; and this it had to do at its earliest convenience, but 'not later than 20th June'. The procedure in making such an application requires plans not only of the Campus itself, but of each building, with floor space, window space, types of materials, etc., clearly indicated. To prepare this data meant, among other things, considerable overtime work. Yet the plans were prepared and forwarded well within the prescribed limit.

As is so often the case in correspondence with the Bantu Education Department, replies are seldom received by return of post. This time six weeks passed and still there was no acknowledgment of our application. Then we were informed in writing that 'apparently our application had gone astray' and we were requested to submit another. So once again we had to go through the process of preparing detailed plans and submitting an application. This time, however, instead of posting the application, I myself took it to the Regional Director in Pietermaritzburg, handed it over to him, and asked him please to forward it to the authorities in Pretoria. The date was 11th August, 1955.

Another six weeks passed, also without any acknowledgment. Then came a telephone message from Pretoria to say that our application had still not arrived. So for a third time we had to prepare plans and submit our application. A week after despatching this third application I phoned to the authorities in Pretoria and inquired if our application had reached its journey's end safely, and I was told that it had.

This delay had now extended over three months and more. Consequently the last quarter of 1955 had come and we were still in doubt as to whether or not we would be allowed to operate in 1956. This uncertainty was a severe trial. What, for instance, were we to tell our students about the coming year? What were we to say to the members of our staff? And what were we to say to those students who were applying for admission for the coming year? What were we to say to our well-wishers and supporters?

On 3rd October we received word by telephone from the Under-Secretary in Pretoria that in view of the late hour and in order not to penalize us for the delay, the Minister of Native Affairs had decided to allow us to continue for one more year on the same financial basis—namely, 75% subsidies for the salaries of the teachers. The Under-Secretary also intimated that no final decision about our future would be made until the members of the Native Affairs Commission had had an opportunity of visiting the College and making their report to the Minister.

On the strength of this communication our Governing Council made three decisions. The first was to accept new students for 1956. The second was to continue with our Appeal for Funds. And the third was to prepare for the visit of the members of the Native Affairs Commission.

One other incident in the closing weeks of 1955 must be recorded. It was a visit in mid-November from the newly appointed Organizers of Industrial Activities under the Bantu Education Department. They came to inform us that we were to admit no new students for our Woodwork Course in 1956, but only students for our Building Course. The reason given for this instruction was that the market for woodworkers was filled to overflowing, whereas the market for builders was great.

These Organizers also informed us that in future all courses in Industrial Schools would be four-year courses instead of three. The reason for this change was not clear, in that no new syllabus had as yet been drawn up or any new techniques introduced. Ostensibly the purpose of this change was to make the students more proficient at their work before they received their certificates. But the reaction in the minds of the students was that they were being called upon to take four years over a course which they could well cover in three.

While these Organizers were at the College two other Government officials, this time from the Labour Department, turned up. These latter came to inform us that we were breaking the law in employing our building students at the Umlazi Glebe, where the College had contracted to build some Native houses for the Durban Corporation. Suffice it to say that, in order to give our students practice in the type of work which they would be required to do after leaving school, we had approached the Durban Native Affairs Department and secured their fullest co-operation in the project of doing some contract work for them, on the same basis as other authorized contractors. I am happy to say that after prolonged negotiation this matter was settled to our mutual satisfaction, and we were permitted to complete our contract work. None the less, this is but another illustration of the difficulties which beset our path.

IV

THE VISIT OF THE
NATIVE AFFAIRS COMMISSION

THE time fixed by the members of the Native Affairs Commission for their visit to the College was the morning of Friday, 1st December, 1955, at 10 o'clock. We looked forward to and prepared for this visit, so great was our shock when only two of the four members arrived. They were Mr W. A. Maree, M.P., and Mr Spies. Accompanying the Commissioners were the Regional Director of Bantu Education, the District Inspector of Schools, and the Professional Adviser to the Under-Secretary.

The representatives of the College were Mr D. C. MacDonald (Acting Chairman of the College Council), Rev. W. R. Booth (Chaplain), Dr Edgar Brookes, Rev. A. F. Christofersen, Mr D. G. Fannin, Q.C., Mr G. C. Grant (Principal), Dr D. G. S. M'timkhulu. Professor Hansi Pollak, Mr D. Rubenstein (Vice-Principal), Dr Allan Taylor, Mr M. Webb, Miss A. Wood and Rev. A. H. Zulu.

On arrival the Commissioners were presented to the College representatives and shook hands with each of the Europeans, but could not bring themselves to do the same with the two African representatives present.

Mr MacDonald welcomed the Commissioners and thanked them for coming, whereupon the College Chaplain offered a prayer.

Mr Maree explained that as this was a meeting of the Native Affairs Commission he would take the Chair. He thanked Mr MacDonald for his welcome and apologized for the absence of the other two Commissioners.

Mr Maree went on to say that one of the aims of the Government was to have all schools for the Bantu handed over to Bantu Communities, as this was considered best by the Government. Though there was provision in the Bantu Education Act for Private Schools, applications for the running of Private Schools would only be considered if special reasons could be presented. He mentioned particularly the Roman Catholics who desired that Roman Catholic children should be educated in Roman Catholic schools staffed by Roman Catholic teachers.

At this point in the proceedings Mr Maree was called to the telephone to speak to the Minister of Native Affairs who was on the line from Pretoria. On his return to the meeting, Mr Maree stated that he desired to hear the College representatives present their case.

Mr D. G. Fannin, Q.C., thereupon presented Mr Maree and his associates with copies of the following Memorandum which were prepared with one main objective—namely, obtaining from the Government permission to be registered as a Private School together with copies of an Annexure rebutting the alleged allegations of the Chiefs and Headmen of the Umlazi Magistracy.

ADAMS COLLEGE

MEMORANDUM FOR CONSIDERATION BY THE NATIVE AFFAIRS COMMISSION

1. The Council of Governors of Adams College are grateful for the opportunity given to a Deputation of Governors to meet the members of the Native Affairs Commission, and to make clear to them the nature of the Association known as Adams College Incorporated, its background, and its reasons for desiring to continue its work in the field of education for the Bantu people.

2. HISTORICAL BACKGROUND

Adams College was founded in 1853 by American Missionaries whose aim was to bring to the Native people of South Africa knowledge and the Christian religion. The Mission Station on which the College was established was originally founded by Dr Adams, who was one of the band of American Missionaries who began their work in South Africa in 1835.

The College has developed along interdenominational lines, and the Articles of Association define the religious policy of the College as 'non-sectarian and evangelical', and provide that official religious services of the College may be conducted by Clergy or Laymen of any denomination or society on invitation by the College authorities.

In 1940, the American Board of Commissioners for Foreign Missions, in conformity with the policy of handing over control, wherever possible, to local bodies, transferred Adams College as a going concern, with all its assets and liabilities, to the Association known as Adams College Incorporated.

This Association is registered as an association not for profit, limited by guarantee, in terms of Section 21 of the Companies Act 1926 (as amended).

Since 1940 the College has been owned by the Association and controlled by a Council of Governors who are elected by the members of the Association and who are bound by the Memorandum and Articles of Association, which have been duly registered with the Registrar of Companies.

During the period since this change took place the Governors have concentrated on building up a good staff, upon putting the College in a sound financial position, in developing its resources, more especially its farm, and upon replacing old buildings and erecting new ones to meet present needs. In spite of a disastrous fire in 1947, when the High School, Training College and Library buildings were destroyed, the Council of Governors have since then succeeded in raising and utilizing over £80,000 for capital needs, and of this about £50,000 has been subscribed by members of the public of all races.

3. THE PRESENT POSITION

As indicated above, the Association which owns Adams College, as well as its Council of Governors, are bound by the terms of the Memorandum and Articles of Association.

The Memorandum sets out its main and paramount object as follows:

'3(1) The main and paramount object for which the Association is established is to acquire control of Adams College in order thereby to maintain and thereafter continue the same in perpetuity as a Christian educational institution for the Bantu people of South Africa and elsewhere and to encourage and assist in the advancement of learning and education among the Bantu people of South Africa, by the establishment or acquisition of schools, colleges, university colleges, or universities, and by any other means whatsoever.'

It is the view of the Governors that this provision imposes both a legal and moral obligation upon the Association to continue Adams College in perpetuity for the purposes set out and that if that becomes impossible of fulfilment, then the Association will have to go into liquidation, its main and paramount object having become incapable of being carried out.

In the event of a liquidation or winding up of the Association, Clause 7 of the Memorandum applies. It reads as follows:

'7.   If, upon winding up or dissolution of the Association, there remains after the satisfaction of all its debts and liabilities any property whatsoever, the same shall not be paid to or be distributed among the members of the Association, but shall be dealt with as directed by the American Board, who shall be given notice of such surplus in writing by the Liquidators by registered post when the amount thereof has been ascertained, provided that if within six months after receipt of such notice, the American Board shall fail to give such directions or if at that time the American Board shall no longer exist in its present or in a modified form, then the said surplus shall be given or transferred to some other institution or institutions having objects similar to the objects of the Association to be determined by the members of the Association at the time of dissolution and in default by the Minister of Justice.'

The Council of Governors which is elected by the members of the Association includes, as at present constituted, both Europeans and Africans. The members of the Association comprise:

(a)   Ex-pupils of Adams College who have reached 21 years of age and who pay an annual registration fee of 2/6.

(b)   Members and ex-members of staff of at least two years' standing.

(c)   Any person or body who has subscribed not less than

£10 to the funds of the Association or of Adams College either before or after incorporation.

(d)   Members and missionaries of the American Board resident in South Africa plus any four other persons nominated by the American Board.

(e)   Persons whose names appear on the Roll of Benefactors (this is not in use).

(f)   Members or past members of the Advisory Board of Adams College as previously constituted.

(g)   Persons enrolled at the invitation and at the pleasure of the Council of Governors.

It will thus be seen that the membership of the Association and the Council of Governors is extremely flexible, and makes it possible for the Bantu to take an increasing part in the control of the College. It has always been the policy of the Council, and it still is, to give increasing responsibility to Bantu members of staff and encourage greater representation of the Bantu on the Council.

The College has always acted in the fullest accord with the Educational Authorities and has always worked in the closest harmony with the School Inspectors. In matters of staffing, curricula, examinations, school calendars, etc., the College has complied with official requirements. To work in accord with the Authorities continues to be the policy of the Council.

It has, we understand, been suggested that Adams College has failed to co-operate with the Government. This is not so, and the decision which the general body of members took, to continue to run Adams College under the existing legislation, should not be interpreted in that way.

Indeed, the suggestion is unfair to a body of responsible people who have for many years been animated only by a desire to maintain Adams College as a place which, by providing a sound education in a community devoted to Christian principles, will continue, as it has in the past, to turn out men and women who will serve their people and their country loyally and with distinction, and who will provide the African people with the kind of leadership which they so badly need.

The Council of Governors, having noted from a study of the Act that Parliament had provided for the existence of Private Schools, considered that Adams College, with its long record

C*

of service to Bantu education, with its flexible and up-to-date constitution, and with a Council which is composed of responsible men and women, must have been the kind of institution which Parliament had in mind. Indeed, the Council goes further, and claims that Adams College, by virtue of the fact that it is an essentially Christian organization and independent of any particular Church, is the ideal type of institution to be recognized as a Private School under the Act.

The Council of Governors, therefore, is quite unable to understand or to accept the charge that it has failed to co-operate with the Government, if that charge is based upon the fact that it has made an election which it was given by the Act, and which the Department, in conformity with the Act, placed before it.

Furthermore, the Governors have been advised that a Resolution was passed by the Chiefs and Headmen of the Umlazi Magistracy on the 14th January, 1955, condemning the action of the Adams Council in closing down the Training College. The answer to these charges is contained in the attached Annexure.

4. THE FUTURE

The Council of Governors desires to carry on the work it has done in the past. It desires to co-operate in that work with the Bantu authorities. Its only purpose is to turn out students who will be able to fit into and to qualify for a proper place in the community to which they belong. As Adams College is a fee-paying school and will continue as such, it is obvious that it will attract a fairly high proportion of potential university students. It would be wrong for the College to fail to qualify such persons to go on to university or to be trained as teachers after leaving Adams College, or if it failed to prepare them for responsible leadership in those spheres.

To that end the Council of Governors asks:

That Adams College be forthwith registered as a Private School, with effect from the date when all subsidies cease.

5. WHY A PRIVATE SCHOOL?

It may be asked why Adams College should be registered as a Private School. The Council of Governors suggests that there are many reasons, the chief of which are:

(1) In a well-balanced educational system there is need for both private and community schools. In the former there is ever the possibility of pioneering in ways not open to the latter. The Department might well find Private Schools most useful in this field. The Governors point to the fact that Adams College has pioneered by being the first College in the Province and in the Union to appoint African Heads of both its High and Teacher Training Schools.

(2) The Council of Governors recognizes the inevitability of the changes in the control and administration of the education of the Bantu People which have been brought about by the Bantu Education Act. The acceptance by the State of responsibility for the main burden of it is parallelled by innumerable examples throughout the world. The Governors believe, however, that by making provision for Private Schools when passing the Act, Parliament recognized that the Private School, of which the only examples among Bantu schools in South Africa were Christian schools, still has a valuable part to play in the new system. It seems unlikely that Parliament had in mind the establishment of secular Private Schools— rather that it contemplated that some of the existing Christian schools would continue to exist.

(3) Adams College is distinctive in that, while its fundamental purpose is to offer a Christian education, it is not controlled by any particular Church and its governing body consists, for the most part, of laymen.

(4) In a specifically 'Christian educational institution' the Christian faith and moral standards are applied throughout its whole community life—in the class-room, on the sports field, in the dormitory, and in the chapel.

To apply such a policy to the whole of the Bantu Educational System would, we recognize, be unfair, and constitute a failure to respect the rights, consciences, and feelings of the non-Christian community, in which category a large proportion of the Bantu people are included. It is, however, still vitally important that there be available to those of them who desire it, and are prepared to make the necessary sacrifice to achieve it, a means whereby their children can be educated in a Christian religious institution, so that the faith which their children have may be integrated into their lives and so that they may demonstrate, in their lives and their service to their fellow-men, the precious truths of the Christian religion.

This is the main and paramount reason why the Association resolved to attempt to carry on its work, and why its members believe that there is room for Adams College as a Private School within the framework of the Bantu Educational System under the Act.

(5) The Council of Governors believes that it is urgently necessary for the welfare of the Bantu peoples, and of the country as a whole, that the Bantu leaders of the future should be imbued with a motivation for selfless service to the community and nation. They realize that such motives are not easily inculcated. It is their conviction that the best way to implant strong motives for service is by integrating Christian faith with education. To do this has always been the aim of Adams College, and it is our intention to continue to serve the country by educating future leaders in this spirit.

(6) A Private School can relieve the heavy burden of Bantu Education in two ways—by taking responsibility for all or part of the cost of teaching from the shoulders of the Department, and by tapping resources both of revenue and of capital which would not be available to a State Department. In this connection, we point to the £50,000 odd which Adams College has raised by private donations in the past seven or eight years, and to the fact that we are satisfied that we can continue to raise the necessary finance in the future, both by way of fees from students, and donations and grants from the public.

(7) Adams College has behind it an enormous body of public support among every section of the community, including Bantu parents and churches. The record of its growth in the past decade, of the constant assistance it has received whenever it has faced difficulties in the past, and the representative nature of its membership demonstrate this.

(8) A fee-paying Private School also ensures that those members of the Bantu Community who can afford to make a greater contribution to the education of their children will be given the opportunity to do so.

(9) The Council understands that the number of institutions applying for registration as Private Schools based on Christian principles is small. Adams College, by reason of its interdenominational character, is fairly representative of the Protestant Christian Churches.

(10) Adams College is no upstart organization, but one with 102 years of service, a responsible body controlling it and a constitution pliable enough to meet the changing needs of a rapidly changing environment. It asks only the right to continue its service to the Bantu people and to train for responsible service and Christian leadership.

Adams College, Adams Mission Station, Natal.   1.12.1955.

In speaking to the Memorandum Mr Fannin made particular reference to the pioneering activities of the College and mentioned, in addition to those set out in the Memorandum, that Adams was the first in Natal to have Matriculation classes for Africans, the first to introduce Mathematics into the curriculum, the first to provide a course for the sons of Chiefs, the first to take a Bantu language on the A Grade, and the first to provide a special Teacher's Certificate.

When Mr Fannin had finished, Mr Maree asked if other members would care to speak. Mr Zulu indicated that there was a real concern on the part of many African parents who had to send their children to boarding schools. He pointed out that so far there were no facilities available under African Community schools. Therefore, the only available Church Schools with boarding establishments would be the Roman Catholic schools. There was, he contended, an urgent need for a school such as Adams which provided a specifically Protestant atmosphere, as distinct from a school in which religion was merely a subject on the curriculum.

The only other speaker at this stage was Dr Taylor of McCord's Hospital, who stressed the need in the medical profession for doctors and nurses with a Christian background, and who were fired with the spirit of service.

Mr Maree then made two points arising out of the Memorandum. He pointed out, in reply to our claim that the College was coming more and more under African control, that the Government had ruled that no European would be employed in any school under a Bantu authority. Secondly, he inquired if it would be possible for Adams to have two separate Governing Bodies, such as a European Governing Board with an African Advisory Board or vice versa. The answer to this question was provided by both Mr Fannin and Dr Brookes, who pointed out that while it might in law be possible to change the articles of the Constitution of the College they could not guarantee that such a change would be acceptable to members of the College Inc. Further, they stressed the practical difficulty of raising funds, for at present Europeans were much better able to make contacts with possible donors than were Africans.

At this stage Mr Maree said that he had some specific questions to ask, and he proceeded to do so.

The first question was whether the Mr A. Luthuli on our Governing Council was the former Chief Luthuli. Mr Fannin replied that Chief Luthuli had been a member of the Council for many years. He made it clear that Chief Luthuli was a member of the Council by virtue of his election, in terms of our Constitution, at our Annual General Meeting three years previously.

The second question related to the parts of South Africa from which the students came. The Principal said that about half came from Natal, and the other half from the other three Provinces of the Union. The third question concerned the reasons for students coming to Adams. The answer was supplied by several speakers, all of whom stressed the esteem in which Adams was held by Africans, coupled with the fact that the children, the grandchildren, and even the great-grandchildren of former students were now applying for admission.

The fourth question inquired if the College authorities were aware that as the College was within a Native Area it might well be classified as a 'White Spot', in which case it would, in accordance with Government policy, have to be removed. Dr Brookes in reply emphasized that there was a marked difference between a European farmer working for his own profit in a Native Area and an educational institution run for the benefit of Africans in a Native Area. He mentioned that this fact was recognized by the Boer Republics before Union, and pointed out that special provision was made in their laws for missionary and educational activities in African Areas.

Mr Maree next intimated that he had seen somewhere that Adams College claimed to give 'a Christian and liberal education'. He desired to know what was meant by a 'liberal' education, and inquired if by any chance it had any connection with the Liberal Party. Here Dr Brookes took the wind out of Mr Maree's sails by replying that 'liberal' before 'education' was spelt with a small 'l', and that as far as he could judge that made an 'ell' of a difference. Even the ranks of Tuscany could scarce forbear to cheer! Indeed, it was the only occasion during the whole interview that Mr Maree and his companions produced a smile.

Mr Maree also intimated that in a Circular letter entitled 'A Message to All Past Students of Adams College' written by a Mr M. T. Moerane who signed himself as President, Adams College Alumni Association, he had noted the sentence: 'Adams College stood for important matters of faith, one of which was that all men are brothers regardless of race and colour and should live as such.' He therefore desired to know the meaning of such a statement. Was it, for instance, a Christian concept of brotherhood or was it preaching the doctrine of a fully mixed society? The answer—and a very unsatisfactory one—was that the Circular had not been issued by the Council.

Now it was that Mr Spies raised his voice for the first time. He ventured to say that it would be unfair to the Bantu if the 'Black Spots' in 'White Areas' were removed and not the 'White Spots' in 'Black Areas'. Both Mr Fannin and Dr Brookes once again went to great lengths to draw the distinction between a white enterprise seeking profit and a white enterprise serving the people. The former was represented by a trader, while the latter was represented by men like Daniel Lindley, who was held in the highest esteem by the Voortrekkers.

Mr Spies also desired to know how many tenants there were on College property, and he was informed that there were no tenants apart from members of staff employed by the College. Not content with the answer, Mr Spies inquired if there were no labour tenants. Once again he was informed that only employees of the College lived on the College property.

Continuing his inquisition, Mr Spies desired to know what

was done with the rents received by the American Board Mission from Africans living on Glebe lands. Though this was not strictly speaking a question for the College to answer, it was pointed out that none of this money accruing to the American Board Mission was turned over to the College. This money was used solely for the purpose of providing educational services for Africans in the Reserves, particularly for the putting up of new school buildings and repairing old ones.

Mr Maree then resumed his questions and this time he addressed his first specifically to me. He asked if I had at any time expressed views against the Bantu Education Act and my answer was the one word 'yes'. Mr Maree then wanted to know if a certain 'Mr A' had been a member of the Adams College staff and, if so, why had his services been terminated. Mr Fannin replied that 'Mr A' had been a member of the staff for only eighteen months and that his services had been terminated because 'it had not worked'. It was purely a question of internal discipline.

Mr Maree next inquired if we were aware of the fact that if we were granted registration as a Private School we would still be subject to inspection. Mr Fannin replied that we were fully alive to this fact and that we were prepared, as in the past, to work with the Government to the best of our ability. Mr Maree also intimated that if it was found on inspection that we were inculcating the wrong type of education, then we would be closed.

Turning to Mr Zulu, Mr Maree asked if he would elaborate more fully his earlier plea for a specifically Protestant Boarding School. Mr Zulu reiterated the concern and desire of many African Protestant parents for a specifically Protestant school. Whereupon Mr Maree asserted that it would be erroneous to think that Community Schools would not have a Christian character. Here Mr Maurice Webb illustrated the matter by reference to his own son, who had learnt Afrikaans at an English School, yet in order that he might be more alive to the whole spirit of the Afrikaner went to an Afrikaans University where he not only learnt the language but imbibed something of its outlook. It was obvious, therefore, that mere provision for religious instruction in the curriculum and even visits of denominational clergy were no substitute for an institution whose chief purpose was to bring up their students 'in the nurture and admonition of the Lord'.

The last question was a mundane one and yet most significant. Mr Maree desired to know what fees were charged by the College and what fees the College proposed charging in the coming year. The answer was that the fees for the current year were £24, while the fees for the coming year would be £28.

Before the meeting ended Mr Fannin drew the attention of the Commissioners to the urgency of an early reply and pleaded that they should take steps to give us their answer to our application without delay. Mr Maree stated that he appreciated our position and he promised to give attention to our plea. Whereupon the meeting was brought to a close with a prayer by the College Chaplain.

At this stage I announced that lunch would be served at my home and that a cordial invitation was extended to all to attend. Within a minute or two of the breaking up of the meeting word reached me that the Commissioners desired me to know that they would not be able to have lunch at my home if the African representatives of the College were present, as it was against Government policy for them to do so. Imagine my predicament. Was I to tell the Commissioners the equivalent of 'to hell with you' and jeopardize all possibility of receiving a favourable reply to our application, or was I to bow to this manifestation of *apartheid*? Happily the situation was saved by the African representatives themselves, who said that they understood the position; and without more ado they went along to my Deputy's home for lunch.

This chapter, however, would not be complete without reference to another meeting attended by the Commissioners that very same afternoon. At this second meeting held at Umbumbulu, barely ten miles away, the Commissioners met the local Chiefs and Headmen, together with representatives of the School Board. Again the purpose of this meeting was to discuss matters affecting Adams College, and once again no official representatives of the College were present. I am informed that the Chiefs and Headmen to a man voted against the College and that a number of others, whether through fear or favour of the Government, did likewise. What then had become of the promise of certain Chiefs and Headmen not to pass judgment on the College before they had heard the College point of view? How hollow was their assurance of their good wishes and prayers! Was it through fear or favour of the Government?

V

THE FINAL BLOW

WHEN the Commissioners left the College on 1st December, 1955, they left with a promise to give our applications their immediate attention. This we interpreted to mean that they would give us their answer soon. Some even thought that their answer would be forthcoming before the close of the year, as there were still as many as thirty days left. But we had failed to reckon with the wiles of Government procrastination.

Christmas came and went and there was no answer; the New Year came and went and there was still no answer. School re-opened in February and again there was no answer. Inquiries of the Head Office in Pretoria were met with the reply that their legal advisers had to be consulted over an outstanding loan to the College. Inquiries of the Commissioners were met with the reply that the Minister had not yet made his decision. Inquiries of the Minister elicited the reply that the Commissioners had only recently presented their report to him and he had not yet had time to study it. And so the matter dragged on week after week, month after month. So when the House rose some seven months after the visit of the Commissioners we were still as much in the dark as ever, in spite of promises from the Commissioners to give their early attention to our plea, in spite of inquiries of the Department, and in spite of a direct question to the Minister.

In the meantime there is another and happier side to our story. First of all, in February 1956, at its biennial meeting, the Christian Council of South Africa passed unanimously the following resolution in favour of the College:

'The Christian Council of South Africa extends greetings

to the Chairman, the Governors, and members of Adams College (Inc.) and wishes them every blessing in their venture to run Adams College as a Christian Educational Institution by registering their High and Industrial Schools as Private Schools. Further, the Council commends this and similar ventures as worthy of the prayers and financial support of churches and individual Christians.'

Secondly, the Pastors' Conference of the Bantu Congregational Church, most of whom were Adams-trained, also passed a resolution in our favour. It read:

'The Pastors' Conference of the Bantu Congregational Church of the American Board, at their annual meeting held at Dweshula Mission Station, Port Shepstone, Natal, from the 30th April to the 6th May, 1956, unanimously resolved to request the Honourable the Minister of Native Affairs to permit Adams College to remain open and to operate as a Private School. The Conference believes that the African people of this country should be allowed to have private church schools as other people do, and that as such Adams can greatly serve the boys and girls who desire a distinctively Christian education. The Conference is confident that Adams will continue to cultivate loyalty and initiative in the students, and to contribute to the progress of Christianity among the African people as well as to their higher academic education.'

And lest it be thought that they gave their support in words only, they had on a previous occasion passed the hat around and sent me the tidy sum of £8 8s.

Another matter of moment was in the month of February, 1956. Miss Janet Lacey of the British Council of Churches, Inter-Church Aid Department, visited the College and held discussions with the College authorities. In March Miss Lacey presented her report to the British Council of Churches and among other things she recommended 'financial support towards an endowment fund for Adams College, primarily for the employment of staff'.

These three events, all within a limited period of time, show that the College had received the blessing and backing of important and responsible church organizations in the country and overseas.

Hardly had this invaluable support come our way than we received from the Action Committee of the Christian Council of South Africa a copy of their report which followed an interview with the Minister of Native Affairs on matters pertaining to the registration and running of Private Schools. Let me quote extensively from the Report, as it reveals clearly the mind of the Minister :

1. The Minister stressed . . . that he had made it clear to the churches that church schools would not be encouraged in competition with Bantu Community Schools . . .

2. There is NO RIGHT within the Bantu Education Act for the establishment of Private Schools but a *privilege* might be given to churches to maintain Private Schools where the Department could not provide adequate schooling . . .

3. Private Schools had been retained in the Act to cover two needs; (a) Where churches had schools before the Act they could continue to operate these schools as Private Schools after the Act came into force (under certain conditions). (b) Where children cannot be housed in Bantu Community Schools, any organization *with its own funds* might be allowed to start a Private School to meet a need.

4. Fee-paying schools were not encouraged and direct fee-paying by parents would not be allowed. Private Schools must be run by special funds.

5. Schools in existence before the Act, which had elected to receive a diminishing subsidy, would be registered as Private Schools when the period of subsidy elapsed at the end of 1957. This registration was almost automatic but it might be affected by a Bantu Community School being opened up in the neighbourhood, in which case the Private School would become redundant. It would also be affected if the Bantu community demanded that the school in their area be a Bantu Community School.

6. There is no guarantee that a Private School once registered would be allowed to continue indefinitely. . . . It could,

however, be closed if there was a strong demand for the establishment of a Bantu Community School. The two would not be allowed to exist side by side or in competition.

7. Virtually NO NEW Private Schools would be permitted.

8. The difficulty about the registration of schools like Adams and Grâce Dieu were that they would only cater for secondary students . . . Private Schools must cater for the whole scale of school needs from Sub A upwards. . . . In the case of Adams strong representations had come from the Bantu people that there should be a Bantu Community School. . . .

13. Such Private Schools as are permitted will have to comply with the syllabus and curriculum of the Department. Such schools will be subject to regular inspection by departmental officers.

14. There is no place in Bantu life for the equivalent of a Private School like Bishops or Kingswood. Denominational boarding schools of this type are not favoured as they draw students from various parts of the country, whereas the aim of the Department is to provide schooling as near home as possible.

About the time that the Minister was granting his interview to the Action Committee of the Christian Council, he was also laying before the House a Bill to amend the Bantu Education Act. This Bill proposed to make two main changes. The first change was that the Bill would empower the Minister of Native Affairs to delegate some of his vast powers to the Secretary for Native Affairs. The second change introduced a new proviso—namely that the registration of any school shall be subject to such conditions as the Minister may determine. In other words, the Minister was seeking yet additional powers —powers to prescribe conditions for any *particular* school without the necessity of promulgating these regulations in the *Government Gazette*, or without these regulations applying to all schools.

When the Parliamentary Session had ended and the Minister had retired to the seclusion of his Pretoria eyrie, there he issued his long-awaited verdict—a refusal to grant us registration.

Phone 37051 x 7   No. 24/302/6915/1

Unie van Suid-Afrika—Union of South Africa
             kantoor van die—office of the
                         DEPARTMENT OF NATIVE AFFAIRS
                         BANTU EDUCATION
                         PRIVATE BAG 212
                         PRETORIA

The Secretary   12.7.56
Adams College Inc.,
Adams Mission Station
NATAL

Dear Madam,
    With reference to your application for the registration of
Adams High School and Adams Industrial School as Private
Schools, dated 11th August 1955, I have to reply as follows:
    After careful consideration the Honourable the Minister
has accepted the recommendation of the Native Affairs Commission that the registration of the schools connected with
Adams College (Incorporated) as Private Schools, cannot be
approved.
    Among the reasons which led to this decision educational
considerations carried the most weight. One is that it is considered essential that the Adams Training School, which was
closed down last year, should be continued as a centre for
teacher-training in this area, and should be re-opened at an
early date. Since at present a training school can operate
only as a government Bantu school, the associated schools
—secondary, practising and industrial—must be classified
either as community schools or as government Bantu
schools.
    The Minister also considers that the door has to be left
open for the Bantu community concerned to assume responsibility for the management of their own schools and school
hostels when they are considered ready to do so. The classi-
fication of these particular schools as government Bantu
schools will be a first step in that direction.
    The Minister appreciates the Council's views in connec-
tion with preparing students for responsible leadership, but

considers that leaders for any particular Bantu community should be produced from within by the community itself, in relation to its needs. A heterogeneous collection of students from all over the country at any particular boarding institution must needs be unrelated to the development of community interests.

Incidentally it is also the Minister's view that European bodies which desire to establish and maintain Private Schools should be prepared to do so with funds from their own resources, and not on the basis of increased school fees. In that Adams College will have to collect fees from the pupils enrolled, at least in part, it fails to comply with this policy.

Assuming that the American Board will be prepared to negotiate in the matter of making its buildings available for school purposes, the Minister envisages the following development at Adams Mission Station:

As from January 1957, the Training School will be re-opened for the training of teachers, and the associated schools, together with the Training School, will be classified as government Bantu schools, with possible reclassification at a later stage as community schools under a Bantu school board.

The hostels will be conducted as Departmental hostels until such time as the Bantu school board may be considered ready to assume control.

Teachers now employed in these schools will be free to apply for appointment under the conditions of service published last year applicable to teachers in government Bantu schools.

The Under-Secretary for Bantu Education expects to be in Durban August 1st, when he will be available for any further discussion the Council may consider necessary.

(Signed) F. J. de Villiers,

for SECRETARY FOR NATIVE AFFAIRS.

My first comment concerns the opening paragraph of the letter. The Secretary for Native Affairs acknowledges receipt of 'your letter dated 11th August, 1955'. This application was the second of our three applications for registration as a Private School. Moreover, it was the one which I had delivered

in person to my Regional Director with the request that he
forward it to Headquarters in Pretoria. You will recall that
after a lapse of six weeks we were informed that this application, like the first, had not been received. Yet here it was,
nearly a year later, being duly acknowledged.

Secondly, the Secretary for Native Affairs claimed that in
arriving at their decision it was educational considerations
which carried the most weight. Arising out of this consideration the Secretary stated that it was essential that the Adams
Training College, which had been closed down the previous
year, should be continued as a centre for teacher training in
the area and should be re-opened at an early date. But at the
close of 1954 our offer to continue to run our Training College
until the Department could make adequate alternative arrangements was turned down on the score that the Government
'would be able to make the necessary provision to maintain
the flow of trained teachers without taking advantage of this
offer'.

The Secretary for Native Affairs further declared that the
door had to be left open for the Bantu community concerned
to assume responsibility for the management of their own
schools and hostels when they are considered ready to do so.
I wonder if the provisions of the Adams Constitution, not to
mention the actual practice of the Adams authorities, did not
leave the door open in a very real sense for the Bantu community to assume more and more responsibility. Indeed the
responsibility given by and provided for at Adams was not
spurious, for it could be assumed when the Africans desired
it, and not merely when the Government considered them
ready to take it on.

In the next paragraph of the Secretary's letter he declared
in almost pontifical terms that 'a heterogeneous collection of
students from all over the country at any particular boarding
establishment must needs be unrelated to the development of
community interests'. How any one who claims to be a South
African and with any knowledge of the history of his country
can make such a statement and expect us to see its wisdom is
beyond me. Surely he does not deny the fact that one of the
glories of his country is its heterogeneous collection of peoples?
For though the Dutch came to this land first, they were soon
followed by a vigorous strain of the French Huguenots. And

when the country came under British rule, the English, the Scotch, the Jews, the Germans, the Americans, and many another added their quota to the South African peoples. Indeed, it would be hard to find a land with a more heterogeneous population than South Africa. And yet Adams is condemned out of hand for gathering together a heterogeneous collection of students under its roof. But we are forgetting— are we not?—that in this land where the Goddess of *Apartheid* is worshipped by those in authority there are different canons of judgment according to race. What is sauce for the goose is not sauce for the gander.

The third and final reason advanced for refusing our application for registration was that we were charging fees. Suffice it to say on this score that there is no boarding school of a similar kind in this country known to me which does not charge fees. To make this protestation even more hollow we only need look at the Prospectus of the new school that has been established at Adams. It says:

' *FEES*: The boarding fee will be not more than £28 per annum payable Quarterly in advance.

The first instalment of £7 must be paid within 7 days of the opening of the College. If the Fees are not paid the student will be sent home.'

It did not take the College authorities long to reply to this letter, and within a few days the following reply was posted:

17.7.1956

The Secretary for Native Affairs,
Department of Native Affairs,
Bantu Education,
Private Bag 212,
PRETORIA

Dear Sir,
I am directed to acknowledge receipt of your letter No. 24/302/6915/1 of the 12.7.56, and to inform you that the decision of the Minister of Native Affairs to refuse our application for registration as a Private School is noted with regret by the Governors of the College.

I am further instructed to advise you that in the interests of the students already enrolled negotiations should proceed apace, as some assurance as to their future is a matter of urgency.

It is considered that preliminary informal talks with representatives of your Department are requisite. Therefore we welcome your announcement that the Under-Secretary for Bantu Education will be available in Durban on the 1st August, for discussion.

In view, however, of the Minister's decision to refuse registration to Adams College to operate as a Private School, the Governors of the College consider that no useful purpose can be served by consultations with them, but that a very useful purpose can be served by consultations at this juncture with officials of the American Board Mission.

The Governors of the College have consulted the American Board Mission and have pleasure in informing you that representatives of the American Board Mission will be available to meet the Under-Secretary on the 1st August.

Nevertheless, the members of the Adams College Governing Council will hold themselves in readiness should the Under-Secretary desire to meet them.

We would appreciate, therefore, if you could communicate the contents of this letter to the Under-Secretary, who we understand is now on holiday—and ask him please to contact us at the earliest date so that arrangements for the meeting can be finalized.

Yours faithfully,
(Signed) J. V. Hosken,
SECRETARY.

In accordance with the final paragraph of the letter from the Secretary for Native Affairs in which he said that the Under-Secretary would be in Durban on the 1st August, 1956, preparations were made for a meeting between representatives of the College, the American Board Mission, and the Government to take place on that day. It was fortunate that at this juncture the Secretary for Africa of the American Board Mission, Dr John Reuling, was in the Union. He was thus able to be present and preside over the discussions.

In order that the position of the Mission should be clarified and not misunderstood, the following statement, dated 25th September, 1956, was issued after the meeting:

'Throughout the present crisis the concern of the American Board has been to make it possible to continue at Adams a Christian school for the benefit of the African people. This is consistent with the purpose for which Adams College was founded, and is in entire agreement with the policy decisions of Adams College Incorporated during the past few years. Under the Bantu Education Act a specifically Christian school could be conducted only as a Private School, run with private funds. Under those circumstances the American Board were prepared to raise from your friends in the churches in America very large sums of money in order to make a private Christian school possible at Adams. But the Minister of Native Affairs has decided not to allow such a school to exist, and he has made it illegal for us to continue after the 31st December of this year. Therefore, in terms of our constitution the college property must now revert to the American Board, and the American Board must decide what to do with it. Full consideration has been given to the opinions and wishes of the association (Adams College Inc.) and of other friends of the College, and the decision has been made that the property should be sold to the Government. This is a very grave decision, and it is the wish of the American Board that the reasons for the decision should be clearly understood by all friends of the College.

'There seemed to be three alternatives open to the Board. The first was to retain the property for other than school uses. It might be used as a conference centre, with the Theological School continuing, and such new activities organized as might be possible. Although this might have much to commend it, the American Board inclined to the opinion that this would not be the best use of the property. Such advice as was available from parents of students and friends of the College, mostly Africans, strongly favoured allowing the Government to conduct a school at Adams, since no one else could legally do so.

'Secondly, the property might have been leased to the Government for a school. Much could be said in favour of

this, and it was at first felt that this would be the right thing
to do. The chief reason for this would be the hope that at
some time in future it might again become possible to
conduct a Christian school at Adams. Obviously this could
be done only if we were in control of the property. And if
there were any reasonable grounds for such hope, the
American Board would quite certainly have decided on this
course. But during the discussions with representatives of
the Native Affairs Department one point became clear
which made it appear improbable in the extreme that we
would ever have real control of the school again. The letter
which informed us of the Minister's decision not to register
Adams College made it clear that he intended conducting
a training college there, for which, we were later informed,
there would be erected a large new building. That building
would be government property, and the Government would
insist on terms of occupation which would prevent the
building from becoming the property of the American
Board as owners of the land. At the same time it would be
an integral part of the College. If we should want to conduct a private school at some future time, when it might be
legally possible to do so, it would be necessary to obtain the
consent of Government to buy their building, and then to
raise a sum of money, running into tens of thousands of
pounds to pay for it. No one has seen any hope that this
could be done. Therefore it is considered that if the Government erect large buildings on the College property, there
will always be a government school there, so far as we can
foresee anything of the future. We are then left with the
question: what is the use of retaining ownership of the
property, if we have no other hope for it than always to
lease it to a government school?

'The American Board are very much concerned that the
work of the Theological School shall not be hindered by
the changes at Adams. For various reasons it seems impossible and undesirable for the Theological School to be
located in a government Bantu school. Therefore, if the
Government operate a school at Adams, it will be necessary
for the Theological School to rebuild elsewhere. This will
involve the building of an entire new school—a very costly
operation. Rent received for the Adams property would not

be enough for this purpose, and it therefore would seem necessary to sell Adams in order to provide new buildings for the Theological School.

'This leads us to the third alternative, which is to sell the Adams property and use the money elsewhere, where we have opportunities to advance the Christian evangelical purposes for which Adams was founded.

'If we sell the property to the Government, what in fact are we doing? In the first place, we are exchanging the immovable property at Adams, which it appears we shall no longer be able to control, for movable property in the form of money, which we shall be able to control and use for the purposes for which the church and mission exist. Such an exchange would seem to be advantageous, and that is the reason why the American Board has consented with regret to the sale of Adams College.

> The American Board Mission Council
> (South Africa)
> (Signed) Samuel T. Kaetzel,
> Samuel T. Kaetzel, Secretary
> 19th October, 1956.'

After a number of meetings and considerable correspondence the method of disposing of the assets of the College, both movable and immovable, was arrived at. By the close of the year Adams College ceased to be and the new government school called 'The Amanzimtoti Zulu College' came into being.

Thus was Adams College liquidated.

THE DUTCH REFORMED CHURCHES IN SOUTH AFRICA AND THE PROBLEM OF RACE RELATIONS

These extracts from a Report of the ad hoc *Commission for Race Relations appointed by the Federal Council of the Dutch Reformed Churches in South Africa, have been reprinted from* The Ecumenical Review, *October 1956 (volume IX, number 1). They afford an insight into the re-thinking which is going on in the Afrikaans-speaking churches of which English-speaking Christians are for the most part unaware.*

CRITICAL REVIEW OF HISTORY

1. From the historical survey it appears that the founding of separate churches sprang from:

   (a) A realization of the cultural and social needs of the non-Whites and a sincere attempt to minister to them more efficiently and to train them for church independence and leadership. 'In all that time there was never any thought of oppression or neglect. On the contrary, as their numbers grew and their buildings and separate congregations multiplied, provision had to be made for their better development and for their acceptance of responsibility and leadership. For this reason the coloured members automatically left the European congregations and established their own congregations, which in 1881 resulted in the founding of an independent Mission Church.' (G.B.A. Gerdener). It is interesting to note that the ministry in separate buildings was undertaken by enthusiastic friends of missions—a proof of the desire to bring the Gospel to the non-whites in the most effective way. This action paved the way for the founding of separate indigenous churches.

   (b) The fact that some European members preferred to

attend separate communion services and to worship independently of the non-Whites. Undoubtedly the motives here were grounded on social and hygienic considerations and on the racial attitudes of the nineteenth century. Possibly the danger of miscegenation played an important part. As early as 1809 there were cases of miscegenation in Graaff Reinet; originally such cases were dealt with in the same way as immorality among Europeans, but afterwards these cases called forth a stronger reaction and stricter proceedings from the Church Council. (TNH in Kerkbode 22 Sept., 1948.)

2. It is clear that the decision of 1857 had only separate places of worship in view, and in this decision there was no intention of excluding the non-White members from the European congregations and vice versa. The present custom in our church, that each racial group is limited to membership of its own church, must be regarded as a result of:
(a) the founding of indigenous churches, each with its own interests and aspiration;
(b) the cultural, social and other differences of the various ethnic groups;
(c) the practice of ministering to the spiritual needs of the non-Whites separately by specially trained missionaries (not ministers) because of differences of language and for other reasons;
(d) the great social and political repercussions of the first half of the 19th century. This must possibly be regarded as the chief reason why the policy and opinion of the Church with regard to this matter underwent such a remarkable change, in the half century between 1830 and 1880.

3. That the decision of 1857 and the founding of indigenous churches, as well as the origin of the custom at that time that members from a specific race could only join their own church, was a matter of practical policy and not of principle, is proved by the following:
(a) The families of European missionaries and other Europeans often worship in the Mission Churches.
(b) The inclusion of two non-White congregations (St

Stephens and Stockenström) in the Mother (European) Church and the presence of their delegated elders at Presbyterial and Synodical gatherings.

(c) The special services at some places which are attended by believers from all racial groups. It is worth noticing that not one of the Federated Dutch Reformed Churches has ever legally or in any other way forbidden the communion of believers from the various racial groups.

DOCTRINAL APPROACH

1. The Dutch Reformed Church can by no means associate itself unreservedly with the general cry for equality and unity in the world to-day. The motives and aims in this connection can certainly not always be regarded as purely Christian. It is mostly a surrogate unity and brotherhood, that men seek to realize without Christ in a world disrupted by sin. It is a futile attempt, because true unity among men can only be realized in Christ.

2. Our Church, however, has true feeling for and a genuine interest in the ecumenical striving of our day. We also believe emphatically that the zeal for this has been enlivened by the Spirit of God with a view to the future. No one, with a true conception of the Biblical teaching on the unity of the Church of Christ, will be able to dissociate himself from this attempt towards a better embodiment and realization of our oneness in Christ. Holy Scripture not only proclaims the holiness of the mystic body of Christ, but also its unity. Not only does it bring a message in the symbolic language of the grapevine and the branches, and the body with many members; it also demands in plain language that we should be one, even as the Father and the Son are one (John 15.4-5; I Cor. 12.14-31; Rom. 12.4-9; Eph. 4.14-16; John 17.21).

3. Indeed the unity need not be brought about artificially; it already exists in Christ. It is to be found in the very nature of the Church of Christ. This nature is not found in the institutionalized or organized Church, which appears in numerous different and often conflicting forms. The nature of the Church is found in the communion of persons united in Christ, over

against the rest of humanity, through faith by the Holy Spirit as members of the same mystic spiritual body. Here we find a unity much stronger and more real, more intense and more dynamic than general friendship or goodwill or co-operation. It is an organic unity of all who, by the Holy Spirit, have been incorporated in Christ. It is a new creation, an organic communion, called the body of Christ (I Cor. 12). Holy Scripture lays especial stress on this communion (*koinonia*).

4. We have here then a supernatural organic communion, which disrupted humanity does not know and which cannot be attained without Christ. It is only experienced by the 'new creature' in Christ. For such 'the middle wall of partition,' caused by sin, has been broken down (Eph. 2.14-16; Col. 3. 10-11). We have here then a unity which cannot be destroyed by the multiplicity of instituted churches or by the derivation of believers from various nations and races. At most the above-mentioned factors can only obstruct the concrete expression of such unity.

5. Because of the depraved and finite nature, also of the people of God, the *Ecclesia* of the New Testament is still, however, imperfectly manifested on earth. Just as this incomplete manifestation displays lack of holiness and power, so also it mars the true realization of the unity of believers. Various factors cause the imperfect realization of our existing unity in Christ, and one of the chief of these is racial contrasts and racial tensions in the world. In South Africa, too, this factor plays no mean rôle. It makes the expression of the unity of believers from different nations and races very difficult. This is, however, true not only of the relationship between Europeans and non-whites, but also of the relationship between all population groups.

6. To an increasing degree the Christian Church is becoming aware of the danger of acquiescing in race relations which may perhaps not be in accordance with the Word of God. Therefore the Dutch Reformed Church is also listening afresh to what the Word of God has to say to us on the above-mentioned matter with respect to the present situation.

D

DECLARATION OF POLICY

It is clear from the above that the present situation is the result of a development or process in the ecclesiastical and social field, which took place in South Africa over a period of more than a hundred years.

The Dutch Reformed Churches now wish to declare that their policy of the past and the present should be understood as follows:

1.   The Dutch Reformed Church accepts the unity of the human race, which is not annulled by its diversity. At the same time the Dutch Reformed Church accepts the natural diversity of the human race, which is not annulled by its unity.

2.   Through free grace God assembles His Church out of all the nations. This assembly of believers or communion of saints forms an indissoluble unity as the mystic body of Christ.

3.   There must be complete clarity as to the nature of the Church and its concrete manifestation on earth. In its essence the Church is the one mystical body of Christ as it exists before God in its spiritual reality. Therefore this unity of the Church must also receive the greatest stress. As opposed to Rome, the Reformers have, however, constantly repudiated the identification of the mystic body of Christ with its institutionary revelation. That, however, does not alter the fact that the unity of the Church remains the Christian ideal.

4.   It is further necessary to have a clear conception of the institutionary revelation of the Church. The co-existence of separate churches resulting from doctrinal differences is a sinful schism, since but one truth and one spiritual reality have been revealed.

5.   This, however, does not mean that the one true Church cannot be embodied in separate independent churches, which in truth confess the Christ of Holy Scripture as their Lord and Saviour.

6.   Even in this diversity of the concrete manifestation of the Church of Christ there is a gradation of attachment and intimacy as a result of natural relationship and common culture. This is expressed, for instance, in the nuances of confession of the same truths as in the *Netherlands Confession of*

Faith and the *Westminster Confession,* which differ only in the phrasing and in the accentuation of the truth.

7. Starting from the unity of the Church of Christ as circumscribed above, and taking the specific racial situation in South Africa into careful consideration, the Dutch Reformed Church maintains the following standpoint as its policy:

(a) That the founding and development of independent indigenous churches for the purpose of evangelizing the native races of South Africa, was both necessary and in accordance with our understanding of the nature of the Church of the Lord Jesus on earth, and has been richly blessed in the many years that have passed.

(b) That since, under the pressure of circumstances, the historical development in the missionary sphere throughout the centuries showed tendencies of un-Christian exclusiveness, thus impeding the realization of the true Christian fellowship between believers, this happened, not through ill-will towards the non-Whites, nor with the approval of the official leadership of the Church, but must be seen as the result of uncontrollable circumstances and of general human weakness.

(c) That in each congregation both the mother- and the indigenous daughter-churches reserve the right to regulate their membership according to the realistic demand of circumstances, and in accordance with the spirit of Christ; but at the same time it is also the Christian duty of the above-mentioned churches to educate their members for and in the practice of a healthy Christian communion of believers, while avoiding any evil motives or annoying and wilful demonstrations.

DECLARATION OF PRINCIPLES

Arising from the above, your Commission recommends that the Churches accept the following principles:

(1) The Creation of God forms a unity which at the same time, however, comprises the richest diversity. (Gen. 1 and 2.)

(2) The unity of the human race is not annulled by its great diversity, which was brought about by the creation and conservation of God. (Gen. 3.20; Acts 17.26.)

(3)   All men are created in the image of God and as such there is no respect of persons with God. In the sense of Creator, God is the Father of all mankind and all men are of equal worth; but in the sense of the New Testament childhood and brotherhood, He is the Father of the believers alone. (Gen. 1.27; 5.1-3; Deut. 32.6; Eph. 6.9; Mal. 2.10; John 1.12; Rom. 8.16; Gal. 4.6.)

(4)   After the Fall, too, God, for the honour of His Name, maintained the unity and diversity of creation by His universal grace. He decreed even greater diversity in order to restrict the expansion of power of mankind in its apostasy and insubordination to Him, and to check the effect of sin in these ways. In His mercy He decreed a multiplicity of tongues and peoples and dispersed and established the human race over the face of the earth. (Gen. 11.6-9; Acts 17.26.)

(5)   Sin, however, has caused permanent schisms in the human race and only some, albeit from all the nations, are ordained in Christ unto the eternal life. (Gen. 4, 5 and 6.1-4; Matt. 25.32; Rom. 9.6 ff.; Rev. 5.9.)

(6)   The Church of Christ, gathered together from all the peoples of the earth, forms a unity, and this unity of his mystic body, the communion of saints (*koinonia*), must always receive the greatest emphasis. Only of these true members of the body of Christ is God the Father in the deeper and more spiritual meaning of the word, and only *they* form a true brotherhood who, through faith in Jesus Christ, have in a special way become the children of God. (Matt. 12.46-50; John 17.21; Rom. 8.15; II Cor. 6.17, 18; Gal. 3.28; Gal. 6.10.)

(7)   The natural diversity and the different spheres of influence and relationship of authority, which God has ordained are in no way broken down by this unity in Christ, but are rather restored and sanctified. This regenerating grace should be especially revealed in the Church of Christ in that the superior or stronger, in full responsibility to God and true love towards his neighbour, will educate and in every respect uplift the inferior or weaker so as to become a worthy fellow-member of the body of Christ. (Acts 2.6-11; Rom. 13.1 ff.; I Cor. 7.17-24; 8.9-13; I Cor. 12; Eph. 4.11-16; 5.22; 6.9; Rev. 21.24, 26.)

The basic rule is valid here, that we should love the Lord our God with all our heart, and with all our soul, and with all our mind, and that we should love our neighbour as ourselves (Matt. 22.37-39). This entails that we shall do nothing through strife or vainglory, but in lowliness of mind each will esteem the other better than himself, and that we, in the practice of unimpeachable righteousness, will give to all what they deserve. (Phil. 2.3; II Tim. 2.22; I John 2.29; 3.10.)

(8) A continual watch should be kept that the unity in the Church of Christ be preserved, in spite of the diversity, and never allowed to degenerate into disruption as a result of sin. (Acts 6.1; I Cor. 3.1 ff.; Eph. 4.1 ff.)

Addendum

Note: The report is followed by an ' Addendum ' from which we quote the following two paragraphs:

This professed unity in Christ in our opinion also demands concrete expression not only between denominations but also between believers of different nations and races. Just as the Church is called to strive after a fuller realization of sanctification, so it is also called to strive after a better experience of the communion of saints. We therefore accept the existence of separate churches according to each indigenous group, but as a matter of principle no person will be excluded from corporate worship solely on the grounds of race or colour.

Because of exceptionally difficult circumstances in South Africa we are aware that the above-mentioned principles can only be applied with discretion and with difficulty owing to the concrete historical situations. The factual situation with which the Churches in South Africa have been faced for many years and are still faced to-day, and the undeniable fact of the power of sin in all human relationships throughout the world, compel the Church of Christ to act carefully in its endeavour to apply these principles in practice. On the one hand this need for careful action explains why only some of these principles have been realized in the past (as the historical survey indicates); on the other hand the Church may not, on these grounds, seek to justify its acquiescence and neglect in this respect.

ANOTHER VIEW

The following passage, illustrating the point of view of a minority in the Dutch Reformed Church, is taken from a lecture given in 1957 by Dr. B. B. Keet, Professor of Theology at the Dutch Reformed Church Seminary, Stellenbosch, on the Ethics of Apartheid.

In human relationships there are natural groups some of which are more closely related to us than others. Beginning with the group into which everyone of us is born, and from which all others proceed (the family), it is evident that the difference between this and other groups—the clan, the tribe, the nation, the race, humanity as a whole—is simply one of the degrees of intercourse; all are associations binding us to our fellow-men and contributing to the formation of our personality. They are associations without which there can be no development of personality. It is also evident that the more circumscribed such an association is the greater the spiritual poverty of its members will be, after the fashion of that caricature of a prayer:

> 'Dear Lord, bless me and my wife,
>   Son John and his wife,
>   Us four and no more!'

The point I wish to make, however, is that whatever influence the group has upon the individual (and it is considerable) moral judgment cannot be passed on the group as such but only on the individual. It is always the individual in the group who is responsible. To treat the group as a magnified individual, apart from its constituent members, is an abstraction that leads to the most disastrous consequences, as is so manifestly proved by the inhumanities of fascism and communism, anti-semitism and colour-prejudice. The plain fact is that group responsibility cannot be defended on an ethical basis unless membership of that group is voluntary, for in the latter case it is not only possible for the individual to dissociate himself from the group, but the group itself can be changed in character and conduct. Even in times of war, the practice of holding a community responsible for the outrages of a few cannot be defended on the grounds of retributive justice. At best it can only be regarded as a punishment designed to act as a deterrent.

In our South African situation we have all the injustices of group-thinking aggravated by the absurd group-formation according to the colour of one's skin. For this difference of pigmentation the individual is held responsible together with his group, as if he had chosen his own ancestors. As a consequence we have developed a caste system which surpasses all others of its kind; because in others it may be possible to advance to a higher caste, but here there is no possibility of change—the coloured man stays coloured even if he becomes the most exemplary citizen of the country. He is one of a group, a mere cipher without any personal attributes or claims.

THE ROMAN CATHOLIC CHURCH

*The following paragraphs are from a joint statement of
the Archbishops and Bishops, in June, 1952.*

The problem, therefore, consists in dealing with:
(a) A deep-rooted prejudice on the part of most Europeans against non-Europeans; (b) On the part of many non-Europeans, resentment and distrust, almost innate in the illiterate and aggravated in the literate through their experiences and reading to such a degree that they can scarcely conceive that Europeans might want to help them to higher attainments; (c) A group of non-European people in various stages of cultural development, of which the majority is still totally unprepared for full participation in social and political life patterned after what are commonly called Western standards; (d) Divisions and animosity between various non-European groups.

The solution to this vexed problem of human relationship can be sought only in prudent and careful planning and in the practice of charity and justice. . . .

There will always be inequalities in society that necessarily affect human relations. These inequalities do not, however, justify behaviour that is offensive and disparaging, for social inequalities in no way detract from the great truth that all men are the creatures and children of God.

Christian charity requires the forgiveness of injuries; it forbids the harbouring of hate, resentment and distrust. Bitterness is no part of charity. Yet charity is not opposed to honest striving for the securing of one's true rights. For charity and justice must go hand in hand. Justice demands that we give every man his due. It is a virtue that prompts us to recognize the rights of others and forbids us to hinder their legitimate exercise. These are rights that flow from the very nature and constitution of man, whatever the inequalities in the natural and social spheres. . . .

If South African conditions are considered in the light of what has been said, one arrives at the following conclusion:

(a) Discrimination based exclusively on grounds of colour is an offence against the right of non-Europeans to their natural dignity as human persons; (b) Though most of the basic rights of non-Europeans are in theory respected, conditions arising out of discriminatory legislation (such as laws restricting employment), social conventions and inefficient administration seriously impair the exercise of these fundamental rights. The disruption of family life is a case in point; (c) Justice demands that non-Europeans be permitted to evolve gradually toward full participation in the political, economic and cultural life of the country; (d) This evolution cannot come about without earnest endeavour on the part of non-Europeans to prepare themselves for the duties connected with the rights they hope to enjoy .

These are the principles that must govern any Christian solution to the racial problem. Charity and justice must supply the driving force, prudence will be the guide. What has been said remains in the realm of principle; it is for men versed and specialized in different branches of study and technique to apply these principles to the difficult and complicated situations.

It will be no easy task. It can be made lighter by the prayers, goodwill and co-operation of all who earnestly desire to see justice and peace reign in this country, and who sincerely believe that it is a Christian duty to love one's neighbour as oneself.

A CONFERENCE OF AFRICAN LEADERS

Passages from a report in The South African Outlook *(November, 1956).*

The African people of the Union of South Africa, at the invitation of the inter-denominational African Ministers Federation, assembled in a national conference in Bloemfontein, from October 4 to October 6, 1956, to consider the Tomlinson report. The representative character of the conference was indicated by the fact that 394 delegates, drawn from all parts of the country, both urban and rural, representing all shades of African political and other opinion, were in attendance.

Careful consideration was given to all aspects of the report, the discussion being preceded by papers prepared by leaders of African thought who are acknowledged authorities in the fields with which they dealt. After detailed examination of the principles and policies enunciated in the report the conference desires to place on record its total rejection of the report as a comprehensive plan for the implementation of *apartheid* in South Africa.

This conference does not subscribe to the view that the choice before South Africa consists only of two alternatives—'ultimate complete integration' or 'ultimate complete separation between Europeans and Bantu'. The conference maintains that a proper reading of the South African situation calls for co-operation and inter-dependence between the various races comprising the South African nation and denies that this arrangement would constitute a threat to the survival of the White man in South Africa.

The conference finds that the net result of the implementation of the Tomlinson Report will be a continuation of the *status quo* and indeed an aggravation of the worst evils of the present system, including their extension to the Protectorates. Under the present conditions the policy and practice of *apartheid* denies the African inalienable and basic human rights on the pretext that the African is a threat to White survival and denies him:

(a) A share in the government of the country;
(b) The inviolability of the home;
(c) Economic rights, the right to collective bargaining and to sell labour on the best market;
(d) The right to free assembly and freedom of travel, movement, and association;
(e) Inviolability of person. . . .

The (Tomlinson) commission looks upon the Church or churches as something to be controlled and used by the government to further its own schemes. The conference disagrees with the commission on the grounds that the churches are the instruments of God for the establishment of His kingdom on earth and, therefore, answerable only to God with a right to intervene in moral issues affecting the nation as a whole. . . .

This conference is convinced that the present policy of *apartheid* constitutes a threat to race relations in the country; therefore, in the interests of all the people and the future of the country, this conference calls upon all national organizations to mobilize all people, irrespective of race, colour, or creed, to form a united front against *apartheid*.

This conference welcomes the initiative of the inter-denominational African Ministers' Federation in bringing together African leaders to consider the Tomlinson Report and its implications for South Africa, and appeals to the Christian Churches in South Africa to take a clear and unequivocal stand in the defence of Christian and human values now being trampled underfoot in the name of *apartheid*.

THE NATIVE LAWS AMENDMENT ACT, 1957

Dr Alan Paton said in Nigeria at the All-African Christian Conference that 'the unity of attitude on the part of the churches (with the exception of the Dutch Reformed Churches) to the famous " Church Clause " of the Native Laws Amendment Act 1957 (which is referred to by Bishop Reeves on page 42) . . . never had a parallel in the history of South Africa. . . . The action of the churches on the " Church Clause " was welcomed with thankful hearts by hundreds and thousands of Christians. Yet the great majority of those people were quiet and law-abiding, the kind of people who give stability to society and support to rulers. Why were they then so ready to follow the lead of their spiritual heads? . . . I believe that many of them were grateful for the reaffirmation of the existence of a spiritual order, and for the reaffirmation of the spiritual authority of the Church. After so many years of legislation which has gravely troubled the Christian conscience, it was a relief to take a stand on an issue so clear and incontrovertible. And let us be in no doubt what the issue was—it was that there is a spiritual realm in which the Church is supreme, and that no temporal authority has a right to intrude upon it. It was at one time a revolutionary doctrine, and indeed might still be called so.'

There follow extracts from some of the declarations of bodies whose attitude has not been otherwise indicated in this book.

THE CHRISTIAN COUNCIL OF SOUTH AFRICA

(representing twenty-three affiliated bodies, and including all the major Churches and Missionary Societies, except the Dutch Reformed and Roman Catholic Churches)

The Christian Council called a Conference of Affiliated bodies at Cape Town on 19th March, which declared:

The conference associates itself fully with the statement issued by the bishops of the Church of the Province of South Africa contained in the letter from the late Archbishop of Cape Town [1] to the Prime Minister.

We take our stand on the following basic rights of religious freedom: the right to assemble for unhindered public worship, the right to freedom of association and fellowship, and the right to preach the Gospel publicly.

The conference further affirms the right of the individual to worship where he pleases and the right of the Church to admit any individual to its services or fellowship.

In making these statements the conference affirms that it would act in exactly the same manner, irrespective of any political party in power which sought to pass a law on the lines of Clause 29 (c) of the Native Laws Amendment Bill.

With great regret the conference asserts that the Christian Churches would have to disregard any laws or regulations which they believe would infringe these fundamental principles.

The conference declares that the denial of freedom of association and the enforcement of compulsory *apartheid* in any sphere of our life is a denial of the law of God and a repudiation of the teaching of our Lord Jesus Christ.

THE METHODIST CHURCH OF SOUTH AFRICA

The following telegram was sent to the Prime Minister, on Tuesday, 9th April, by the President of the Conference and the Chairmen of Districts of the Methodist Church of South Africa, assembled in Durban:

'AFTER LONG AND CAREFUL SCRUTINY OF CLAUSE 29 (C) AS AMENDED OF THE NATIVE LAWS AMENDMENT BILL WE THE APPOINTED LEADERS OF THE METHODIST CHURCH OF SOUTH AFRICA REPRESENTING OVER A MILLION SOULS ARE CONVINCED THAT THERE IS

[1] The signing of this document on 6th March was the last act of Dr G. H. Clayton, who died suddenly on 7th March.

NO JUSTIFICATION OR NECESSITY FOR THE CLAUSE STOP NOTWITHSTANDING THE MINISTER'S ASSURANCE THAT INTERFERENCE WITH RELIGIOUS LIBERTIES WILL NOT BE EXERCISED WE ARE PERSUADED AND ADVISED THAT THE CLAUSE DOES NOT PROTECT THE CHRISTIAN CHURCHES AND PEOPLE FROM ARBITRARY ACTION BY STATE AUTHORITIES STOP THE PROTECTION WHICH THE MINISTER STATES IS NECESSARY IS ALREADY ADEQUATELY PROVIDED FOR IN COMMON LAW STOP WE THEREFORE URGE THE WITHDRAWAL OF THE CLAUSE.

The subsequent amendment to the clause in no way overcomes our objection. . . . We wish to emphasize that the Methodist people are a law-abiding people, but if this legislation places us in the position where we have to choose between obedience to the State and obedience to God, we reiterate that our choice is clear. 'We must obey God rather than man.'

THE BANTU PRESBYTERIAN CHURCH OF SOUTH AFRICA

This statement is to associate the Bantu Presbyterian Church of South Africa, the great majority of whose ministers are Africans, with the protest of the South African Christian Council against the passing of the clauses in the Native Laws Amendment Bill, which empower the Minister to prohibit the attendance of Africans at religious services in European urban areas.

Such legislation, restricting religious liberty, can mean that Africans in domestic service in European residential urban areas, who at present can in some places attend Sunday services in European church buildings, could be debarred from doing so, and would thus be debarred from attendance at any Sunday worship, as in most such areas there are no African church buildings.

Further, such legislation will encourage the mistaken belief, far from dead among some Africans, that there is one God for

Europeans and another for Africans. The result of such legislation can only be to weaken the work of Christian churches
and missions among Africans, particularly the more material-
istic and primitive among them. This can hardly be the purpose
of a Christian Government.

29.3.1957.   D. V. SIKUTSHWA, *Senior Clerk*.

SPECIAL RESOLUTION

OF THE

SEVENTY-FOURTH ANNUAL CONFERENCE

OF THE

METHODIST CHURCH OF SOUTH AFRICA

OCTOBER, 1956

STATEMENT ON PUBLIC AND POLITICAL QUESTIONS

THIS Conference of the Methodist Church of South Africa, assembled at Cape Town, declares what it believes to be the will of God on some of the public and political issues of our day in South Africa.

(1) *Growing Social Concern*

We express our gratitude for the evidences of a growing public opinion and concern, often unaided and self-inspired, regarding such matters as the care of the aged, the need for organized planning for mental health, the treatment of alcoholism, and the provision of more adequate opportunities for the care of retarded children. It is a matter of great important that many such organizations are bringing new hope and courage to young and old alike.

(2) *Race Relations*

We protest emphatically against the enactment, and anticipated enactment, of laws which we regard as unjust, unchristian, and inhuman. The enforcement of the Group Areas Act even thus far has brought acute distress and utter hopelessness to those ejected and the thousands whom it is proposed to eject summarily from their homes. Additional to this iniquitous Act, with its harsh ramifications into practically every phase of African, Coloured, and Indian life, we might quote such unjust measures as:

> The Natives Prohibition of Interdict Act;
> The Industrial Conciliation Act;
> The Natives Administration Amendment Act;
> The Natives (Urban Areas) Amendment Act;
> The Nursing Amendment Bill;
> The Population Registration Act;

which, with others, regiment human beings and turn men and women into cyphers in a manner found in no other than a Police State.

We could cite other measures and scores of cases, emphasising the way in which they are even now causing the most acute distress to individuals and communities, not infrequently taking away the very means of livelihood they have hitherto enjoyed. We place it on record that we regard these laws, directed in many cases against *all* Races in the Union, but mainly of a harsh, inhuman nature towards the under-privileged and helpless (without whom the country could not possibly be run); also the delegation of powers altogether dictatorial to individual men as likely to err as many of us, with utter repugnance. We refer particularly to powers given to Ministers and subordinate officials to deprive individuals of liberty of speech, movement and assembly without open trial or redress by the Courts.

We would urge the responsible Government departments to take serious account of African Christian opinion expressed so clearly in the recent deliberations in Bloemfontein. It is our judgment that no responsible body can afford to ignore the commendably patient and tolerant demands of such representative opinion on the part of moderate African leadership.

(3) *Christian Civilization*

We note the reiteration by many of our political leaders that the aim of their policy is to save white or western civilization, but it appears to us that by their deeds many of them are, in fact, destroying it. We believe that it is much more important to make our civilization Christian than to make it ' white ' or ' western '.

(4) *Family Life*

We note with satisfaction the growth and development of the movement for the strengthening of family life and the setting up of marriage guidance councils in various centres. We would stress the significance of the situation in which the great majority of children in our institutions are neither orphans nor from very poor homes, but the apparently unwanted offspring of divorced parents. We call for a greater effort to assist those who are facing marriage difficulties too complex for them to overcome unaided, and we commend to all who are able to undertake it the work of trained marriage counselling.

(5) *Crime and Delinquency*

The increase of juvenile delinquency, the growing number of crimes of violence, particularly in urban areas, reports of brutal treatment meted out to African people, the toll of death and severe injuries sustained in road accidents, and the alarming increase of alcoholism, are not only cause of deep concern, but a challenge to our conscience. We urge those in authority to intensify their efforts to bring about reformation and rehabilitation. In this regard we call for a careful reconsideration of the policy of whipping as a deterrent to crime, since comparative statistics clearly show that it has failed to achieve the desired result, as well as being degrading both to those who administer and those who receive the punishment.

(6) *State Lotteries*

We take note of the continued agitation for the establishment of a state lottery in South Africa, and reiterate our view that such a measure, which we would vigorously oppose as a Church, would be detrimental to the best interests of our land and people.

(7) *Mutual Goodwill*

We believe that whilst the Church must be fearless and forthright in its denunciation of evil in every form, no one Church party or group has a perfect policy to meet the needs of our times. It is imperative that we seek to understand one another's point of view and join together wherever possible in order sincerely to do what we believe to be the will of God in the present situation. We therefore call upon all sections of the community to seek the path of Christian reconciliation, harmony and goodwill.

POSTSCRIPT FROM GREAT
BRITAIN

'The fact that we are multi-racial is a fact of history. It is an act of God. Multi-racial is not a term of abuse. It is a challenge to our ethics and, above all, to our common sense. If South Africa lacks the common sense to deal with the problem, the world will suffer no undue loss as the result of our disappearance.

It is also a challenge to our leadership. It will indicate who are our leaders and statesmen, and who are merely demagogues and politicians. That applies to the Afrikaans and English-speaking groups and it applies to the Bantu.

We must choose between the call of South Africa and the call of the group.'

These are the concluding paragraphs of the very important little book by Professor P. V. Pistorius, Professor of Classics at the University of Pretoria.[1] In the introduction, he had remarked that while we praise the 'men of simple faith and freedom-loving spirit' who pioneered in the dangers of a wild and new country, we forget that most probably they faced these dangers because of their 'inability to face the problems of human relations' in the countries they had left, and had in particular drawn our attention to the failure in human relations of the Boers and the English in the nineteenth century which had led to the great trek northwards from the Cape. 'But there is no further trek. Hate, unless arrested, must take its course. We are like heroes in some classical drama. We see our own doom inevitably approaching, but we are powerless to avert it. And it is a doom of our own making. Those whom the gods wish to destroy, they make insane. What gods have made the various groups in South Africa blind and insane? God could not have done so, since he has revealed himself to the world as God of love. But the gods of our own making have that power. He who creates a tribal god, will perish by the tribal gods of others. He who worships his own

[1] P. V. Pistorius: *No Further Trek* (Central News Agency Ltd., South Africa, 1957).

116

group and regards even injustice as good if it is thought to be in the interests of his group, will perish by the injustices perpetrated by other groups.'

These are passages from a book which analyses in successive chapters the pattern of fear by which each group—English-speaking, Afrikaans-speaking, Coloured, Bantu—is obsessed and paralysed, and appeals to them all as South Africans to face together the problems which they must solve together if they are not to be engulfed together in a common ruin. It is an appeal by an Afrikaans-speaking South African to all South Africans.

Most of those, I suppose, who will read this book are not South Africans; but that does not and cannot mean that we are safely on the sidelines. If we are citizens of the United Kingdom, have we considered Anglo-Boer relations in the last century? Have we remembered that world opinion was as against us at the time of the South African War at the turn of the century as it was at the time of Suez a year or two back? Have we reflected on the way in which the point of view of Botha and Smuts has been discarded by their fellow-Afrikaners, and wondered whether British administrators, Lord Milner for example, and British policy in general, may have some responsibility?

I am not suggesting that because we all in some sense share some responsibility and guilt, we are precluded from making a judgment or taking a stand. The structure of this book makes it clear for example that I agree in general with Bishop Reeves and with the authors of the protests against the successive acts of the Nationalist Government of the Union of South Africa, and wholly reject *apartheid* as an ideology and as a policy. But surely in honesty this stand must be taken not in self-righteousness but in penitence. Surely the point of the Gospel is that sinful men are justified, that God calls and can use sinners, that a man in Christ is, in the Reformation phrase, *simul justus et peccator*, at once right with God while yet a sinner.

We are not called on to repent the sins of others but our own. And they are not all matters of history. In Birmingham (England) or Birmingham (Alabama) for example, are we happy about the pattern of race relations, about the integration of black and white and brown into what must become even in our countries in some sense a multi-racial society? Is there not some danger that some of the indignation which is aroused in other countries by acts of the South African Government is a psychological mechanism for exporting our disquiet about race relations in our own cities? Is it not easy for Englishmen and Anglicans (such as I) to blame everything on the Afrikaners, and to overlook both that there is an increasing disquiet among Afrikaners, and opposition too, to the policies of 'their' Government, and also that what Bishops and Synods *say* is not necessarily the same as what the mass of Church-people *do*? As Professor Pistorius remarks, 'It would be unrealistic to think that English-speaking South Africans on the whole favour the open-door policy with equal political and economic rights for the various colour groups in the country.'

Let us take, then, the stand for right to which we believe we are called, and take it in penitence for our share in the pattern of fear, and not in self-righteousness. And let us, thirdly, take our part in the ministry of reconciliation. As I write, it appears probable that the Nationalist Party will win the General Election which is to be held in a few days' time. If it does not, and the United Party is returned, the possibilities of reconciling action will be greatly enlarged, and the urgency of action thereby increased. But either way, we are called to share in the ministry of reconciliation of Christ, remembering that the Apostle who gave us that phrase was also the apostle who withstood Peter and Barnabas on a point of principle to the face and was also the writer of I Corinthians 13. And even if the doom which Professor Pistorius and others see looming over South Africa does finally overwhelm all the groups, there will *still* remain the need to maintain or to restore human and Christian relations in and after disaster.

D.M.P.

THOUGHTS AND PRAYERS

I am proud of my colour; whoever is not proud of his colour is not fit to live.

You can play some sort of a tune on the white keys of a piano; you can play some sort of a tune on the black keys; but to produce real harmony you must play both the black and the white keys.

Some white men ought to be transformed into Negroes just for a few days so as to feel and suffer what we suffer.

J. E. Kwegyir Aggrey, of Achimota

AFRICAN FELLOW

Cry a halt in the bitter journey:
   The prisoner's stumbled, He's lying prone.
Beat Him up again! He can't make it;
   He can't carry the weight alone.

Pair of strong shoulders there in the roadway—
   'Here, you, black-face, time's getting late;
Give us a hand with this awkward cross beam . . .'
   African fellow shoulders the weight.

Shoulders the weight and keeps following after,
   Can't see the Face of the Man before;
Feels the wood bite into his shoulder,
   Grips it tighter and sets his jaw.

All the length of the dusty roadway,
   All the struggle to mount the hill,
African fellow sticks close to Jesus—
   Some of us know he's doing it still.

Yes, and today Christ needs those shoulders,
   That stubborn patience, that strength to bear;
The Cross is there and it's grim and heavy,
   And men shrink back in their pride and fear.

But the African fellow keeps coming forward;
   He can't see much, but he knows the Man.
Despised, rejected, he knows the burden,
   He faces the taunts as only he can—

African fellow, you make us shamefaced;
   You have travelled a road we have never seen;
You have borne the weight in the dust and anguish,
   You and your Lord, and the Cross between.

MARGARET CROPPER

THE CRUCIFIXION

Oh! Mighty God. Oh! Mighty God
Who hast the strength of many waters,
The strength of thunder and of storm
   Oh! Thou art the Mighty One—
     Thou art Eternally.

You can see! Yes! He is carrying our sins.
On that Mount of Calvary.
See! Oh! He is crucified between two robbers
   Father!
     Thou art Eternally.

And as Jesus looks down and sees—
Oh! Yes! he sees
His Mother Mary and His loving John,
He says, 'Mother, behold thy Son',
   'Son, behold Thy Mother'.
     Oh! Father!
   Thou art Eternally.

Our Lord looking into the heavens,
As he hangs upon the mighty Cross,
Says with a loud, loud voice—
   'My God! My God!
   Why hast Thou forsaken me?'
His head, yes! Jesus' head drooped
   And Jesus died.

So through all the length of days
He died a willing death.
   Truly! Truly! Father in Heaven
     Thou art Eternally
      The Alpha and Omega.

                    JEREMIAH MONKOE

THE BLACK CHRIST

If aught of worth be in my psalms,
It in the Black Christ's Hands I lay,
In those Nail-grooved, hoe-harden'd Palms
He holds to me now ev'ry day—.
The Black Christ in Whose Name I pray,
Yet Who (O wonder!) prays to me
In wrong and need and contumely.

If any gift of sight of mine
Our land's veil'd beauty should reveal,
My reader, to those eyes of thine,
That gift to Him that gave assign,
To Him (whose Feet unsandalled steal
Over the granite tracks I tread)
Head-haloed by our rose and grey
Of twilights, or our gold of day.

Who near my red camp-fire will spread
His reed-mat, or on rain-bless'd days
Hoe deep His pattern-work of praise
Full in my sight.
              O happy eyes
Are mine that pierce the black disguise
And see our Lord! O woe of woe
That I should see, that I should know
Whom 'tis they use that use Him so!

ARTHUR SHEARLY CRIPPS

THE LITTLE BLACK BOY

My mother bore me in the southern wild,
And I am black; but oh, my soul is white!
White as an angel is the English child,
But I am black, as if bereaved of light.

My mother taught me underneath a tree,
And, sitting down before the heat of day,
She took me on her lap and kissed me,
And, pointing to the East, began to say :

' Look on the rising sun : there God does live,
And gives His light, and gives His heat away,
And flowers and trees and beasts and men receive
Comfort in morning, joy in the noonday.

' And we are put on earth a little space,
That we may learn to bear the beams of love,
And these black bodies and thus sunburnt face
Are but a cloud, and like a shady grove.

' For, when our souls have learned the heat to bear
The cloud will vanish, we shall hear His voice,
Saying, " Come out from the grove, My love and care,
And round My golden tent like lambs rejoice." '

Thus did my mother say, and kissed me,
And thus I say to little English boy.
When I from black, and he from white cloud free,
And round the tent of God like lambs we joy,

I'll shade him from the heat till he can bear
To lean in joy upon our Father's knee;
And then I'll stand and stroke his silver hair,
And be like him, and he will then love me.

WILLIAM BLAKE

THOU, THOU, THE GREAT ONE

This is he the great God, high in high Heaven,
Thou, thou, the Great—Great One, of Truth
    the Buckler,
    Thou, thou, the All Glorious, of Truth the
      Stronghold,
Thou, thou, the Great—Great One, in whom
    Truth shelters,
    Thou, thou, the Almighty, high in the highest,
Thou who hast created life all about us,
    Created the heavens domed far above us,
Created the star-worlds, pure shining.
    Our eyes stared, blinded, until he taught us;
Thou madest us blind, it was thy purpose.
    With the blast of a trumpet, he gave us the
      message
As he hunted to find us, sought for our spirits,
    Sweated hard in his labour to turn foes to brothers,
Thou who art our Leader, thou who dost guide us.
    The robe from his shoulders he cast about us,
Thy cloak, O Saviour, whose hands are wounded,
    Thy cloak, O Saviour, whose feet are bleeding.
See the stream of his life blood that floweth
    to save us,
    That floweth to save us though we did not ask it.
Is it paid so freely without our praying,
    Heaven our homeland with no beseeching?

NTSIKANA, A BANTU CHRISTIAN

FOR FAITHFUL WITNESS

O GOD, who didst call thy servants the missionaries and martyrs of Africa to be thy faithful witnesses, and by their labours and sufferings didst raise up a people for thine own possession: Shed forth, we beseech thee, thy Holy Spirit upon thy Church in this land, that by the sacrifice and service of many thy holy name may be glorified and thy blessed kingdom enlarged; through Jesus Christ our Lord, who liveth and reigneth with thee and the same Spirit, ever one God, world without end. Amen.

Book of Common Prayer:
Church of the Province of South Africa

FOR STRUGGLING RIGHTLY

O GOD, you are the God of all the earth and the heavens. We are so insignificant. In us there are many defects. But you know all about us. For coming down from Heaven you were despised and brutally treated by the men of those days. For those men you prayed because they did not understand what they were doing, and that you came only for what is right. Help us to struggle in that way for what is right. O Lord, help us who roam about. Help us who have been placed in Africa and have no dwelling place of our own. Give us back a dwelling place. O God, all power is yours in Heaven and Earth. Amen.

Hosea Kutako

FOR INTEGRATION

O LORD Jesus Christ, who was born of a Hebrew mother yet rejoiced in the faith of a Syrian woman and of a Roman soldier, who welcomed the Greeks who sought thee and suffered an African to carry thy cross, help us to bring men of all races to be fellow heirs in thy Kingdom.

A prayer regularly used in Zululand

ACKNOWLEDGMENTS

A hymn by Ntsikana, a Bantu Christian, is from Daniel J. Fleming: *The World at One in Prayer*, published by Harper & Brothers.

A Prayer by Hosea Kutako, is from John Gunther's *Inside Africa*, published by Hamish Hamilton.

'If aught of worth be in my Psalms' is by Arthur Shearly Cripps and was first published by B. H. Blackwell.

'The Crucifixion' by Jeremiah Monkoe, is from *Cyrene*, by E. G. Paterson, published by S.P.G.

'African Fellow' is by Margaret Cropper.